D1259035

DEEP WATERS

GOD'S INVITATION TO GO DEEPER

GABE
JENKINS

Deep Waters: God's Invitation To Go Deeper

Gabe Jenkins

Library of Congress Control Number: 2014908251
Copyright © 2014 Gabe Jenkins

ISBN: 978-0-9903023-0-8

Edited By: Jim Kochenburger
Cover and Interior Design By: Janelle Evangelides

DEEP WATERS

God's Invitation To Go Deeper

I dedicate this book to my children: Avery, Sophie, and Owen. May you always venture deeper with God.

INTRODUCTION

I've been dreaming about this moment for a long time. I'm standing on the shore of the Pacific, looking out upon the endless miles of expansive ocean. The sound of the waves brings a smile so large it rivals the stretch of the horizon. I take my first step into the frigid waters and every cell in my body is called to attention. I didn't expect the water to be this cold, but the adventure that calls is worth the temporary feelings of discomfort.

The ocean floor is a gradual slope leading to a steep drop-off several hundred yards off shore. That's where I'm headed, but the sting of the cold water only intensifies as I venture deeper. I glance back at the beach to see several people gathered. They're not carrying boards; they just came to watch. They seem to be comfortable, smiling, carrying on in conversation as they watch thrill seekers chase waves.

As a young boy growing up in the landlocked state of Kansas, I could only dream of what it would be like to ride upon the power of the ocean, to surf. The only waves in Kansas are waves of golden brown wheat oscillating in the wind. Today, my opportunity has finally arrived.

Less than twelve months before, I had compiled a list of ten desires I wanted to see fulfilled this year. Near the top of my list was surfing. I prayed a simple prayer and asked God if He would provide the opportunity. I had all but forgotten about this prayer when my brother called a few months later to extend an invitation to join him on a surfing weekend near Monterey, California.

Excitement filled my soul as I realized my prayer was being answered. I booked my plane ticket, and followed that with a quick Internet search of prime surfing locations near Monterey. I wanted to see the waves for myself, so I typed in "surfing near Monterey" on YouTube. The first video that appeared was from a local news station, and the story was about a man who had just been attacked by a shark in the very waters we would be surfing.

That story is replaying in my mind as I sit on the board with my legs dangling into the murky ocean. Now in fairly deep water, I can't see anything that may be swimming around me. My imagination is kind enough to start playing the theme song from *Jaws*. The chattering of my teeth reminds me I'm still cold. Perhaps the spectators gathered on the beach were the smart ones. I force my attention back on the waves and remind myself why I've come. After several minutes of letting smaller waves pass beneath my board, I decide to go deeper. I'm paddling through thick seaweed, but the allure of the larger waves beckon me to keep going.

Now I'm in the ideal spot. I turn my board around and look over my shoulder, waiting for the power of the ocean to sweep me up, and with a smile on my face and hair blowing in the wind, gloriously usher me to shore while the gallery of spectators cheer me on.

I see my wave and start paddling. I let out an excited holler as I feel the initial surge. I try to pop up on my board, but I quickly lose my balance and smack my face hard against the water. Not exactly what I had in mind. I can picture the gallery laughing. Perhaps that's why they sit on the beach—they want to see others wipe out. It's OK, though, because I'm in deep water. This is where adventure happens.

SPIRITUAL SPECTATOR

For years, I was a spectator on the beach. I watched others live with great faith and follow Christ into deeper spiritual waters, but I was comfortable in knee-deep water. This was just enough to make me feel like I was a Christian, but I still maintained complete control. Anytime God beckoned me to go deeper, the sting of discomfort and the fear of the unknown refocused my attention back to shore and the pleasant activities I enjoyed.

All this time on the beach was creating a sort of sunburn—I was having fun in the moment, but I didn't realize I would experience the pain of the burn later. In other words, shallow water was dangerous for me. In my boredom, I became fascinated with all the wrong things. To create my own entertainment, I started living a lifestyle that wasn't congruent with what God wanted. This provided momentary bliss as I forgot about the dull ache in my soul, but I couldn't run forever.

God continued to call. Richard Foster captured my experience well by writing:

Perhaps somewhere in the subterranean chambers of your life you have heard the call to deeper, fuller living. You have become weary of frothy experiences and shallow teaching. Every now and then you have caught glimpses, hints of something more than you have known. Inwardly you long to launch out into the deep.1

I finally hit my knees on a cold, January night and came face-to-face with the reality of my life. I surrendered to Jesus. I told Him that I can't live this way anymore. The days of calling myself a Christ follower while rejecting the reach of His hand were over. I prayed a simple prayer: *Take me deeper, Jesus.*

God surely answered that prayer, and it's been quite a journey. I had no idea what I was missing out on; the richness of life and the abundance of joy and peace that were available through a deeper relationship with God. This book was birthed out of a simple desire to help others discover the same. Whether you're still not sure about the idea of faith, or if you've been walking with Christ for decades, the call is still the same: *Come deeper.*

My prayer is that you don't read this book like you would a recipe book, looking to be told exactly what to do in order to create a deeper relationship with God. Your walk with Christ was never intended to be a cookie-cutter journey that looks exactly like someone else's. God is far too mysterious for that kind of simplicity. However, there are some overarching ideas that are true about your journey as well as mine.

First, we're invited to know Jesus intimately. We are not called to simply know about Him, but He wants us to *know Him*. This is actually possible. He wants us to learn to recognize what He's doing in our lives on a daily basis, to learn to hear His voice, and to possess a radical obedience as we set our sights on following Him.

As we follow, He'll surely lead us into the deep water of the Father's heart, which is the focus of the second section of this book. Jesus always has been and always will be passionate about revealing the Heavenly Father. He wants you to experience the same love He experienced. This love originates in the heart of the Father, and Jesus wants to take you there. We'll discover a matchless level of love that can't be adequately translated into words—we're just left to experience it. We'll find a generosity and level of kindness that draw us even closer to God. We'll discover more and more of the wonder and privilege of being called sons and daughters of this perfect Father.

As the great Scottish writer George MacDonald stated, "Because we are sons of God, we must become sons of God." The third section of this book probes how Jesus leads us into the deep water of our own hearts. This journey is designed to bring a greater revelation of our identity. He'll help us align our lives to reflect the truth of what we carry in our redeemed hearts. After all, we've been created to bear the image of a glorious God, and we glorify Him most when we live from the heart.

Finally, the fourth section of this book will explore how Jesus guides us into the deep and living waters of the Spirit. He wants us to drink from the only fountainhead that can truly satisfy—the Spirit of God. He wants to see us become people marked by His distinguishing presence and living lives of power and purpose. This is the heritage for the people daring enough to push off from shore and follow Him into the deep.

Won't you come along?

SECTION I
DEEPER WATER

Put out into deep water...--Jesus

"WHAT YOU CAN'T SEE"

I'm writing this on a Saturday night. I think I have a fairly good idea what tomorrow will hold. I'll wake up early, pray, eat a bagel, kiss my wife, go to church and serve as a pastor, come home and eat a sandwich, rest, play with my daughters, go back to church for the evening service, and finish the day watching ESPN. It should be a good day: the status quo for Sunday.

Why do I make this mistake and think I know exactly what tomorrow will hold? It's almost as if I live life on cruise control at times, assuming today or tomorrow will look like yesterday and the day before. The more I talk to people, the more I realize I'm not alone in making this assumption. Don't we all kind of have a feeling of what today will be like? What about Monday? We wake up with a sigh and think, *God, help me get through this day.* Saturday morning? You probably don't wake up with a groan, but I'm sure you have a fairly good idea of what you think the day will hold. We are creatures that like to settle into routines—nice, comfortable, safe routines.

While effective planning and establishing routine are good things, we must not allow ourselves to lose an eager expectation for God to surprise us, to break in and fully have His way each and every day. What if we would wake up in the morning, and instead of immediately thinking of all that needs to be accomplished, surrender ourselves completely to the story God is telling? What if we approached each day as a blank canvas in the hands of a brilliant artist? (The extravagant sunsets in the western sky provide continual evidence of God's artistic ability.) I've learned over the years that God is a masterful storyteller, and He's telling a story through each of our lives.

My favorite aspect of counseling is listening to a person's story. Everyone has a unique story, but we live in a culture where we rarely pause to view our lives through this lens. We're too busy. We have too much to do. All we often have time for is to casually ask, "How are you doing?" The other person will predictably say, "Good. How are you?" The entire exchange lasts less than two seconds, and it's painfully awkward.

Meanwhile, as we hurry along, God taps us on the shoulder and whispers, "I have more for your life. Are you willing to live my story?" My heart speeds up a few ticks as I ponder the invitation in a fresh way. Even after being a Christ follower for decades, I still get nervous about not knowing the details of this grand story. At the same time, I'm intrigued. The mysteriousness of God as Author causes me to lean in. Don't we enjoy a movie more when we don't know the ending? We're rarely on the edge of our seat if we know precisely what is about to happen on screen.

How much more should we be on the edge of the seat with our own story? What is God going to do next in and through you? We are talking about the Author who starts the story by breathing the galaxies into existence. His creativity and ability to do the unthinkable is indescribable—even on Mondays.

So, why aren't our lives more exciting and fulfilling? Perhaps it's because the tap on the shoulder has been overlooked because the world is shoving us along. God's whisper has been drowned out by the demands of the day. Or maybe we are simply too comfortable on the beach—or in the stands—watching other people live great stories.

THE COURAGE TO PARTICIPATE

I've never met him, but I can't help but admire Lionel Rodia. He is a middle-aged man from Philadelphia who is a die-hard Phillies, 76ers, and Eagles fan. He also possesses an uncanny ability to maneuver his way into prestigious sporting events—like the way he got into Super Bowl XXI without a ticket. Once in, he slowly but surely laid claim to some of the best unused seats in the house.

His crowning achievement occurred during game five of the 2008 World Series. He initially found himself sitting near the left field foul pole, but it wasn't long before he made his way to the Diamond Club section and enjoyed the rest of the game two rows up from home plate.

As good as *his* new seats were, he wasn't satisfied remaining in the stands. When it became evident the Phillies were going to win the game, thus clinching their

World Series title, Lionel began plotting a way to join the players in celebration. When the time was right, he stood up and followed an important looking man into a special back room where he found himself in the company of Bud Selig, several other men in suits, and the World Series trophy. Lionel then fell in line and followed them onto the field where people continued to assume he was somebody affiliated with the team. They gave him a championship shirt and even placed a lei around his neck while he high-fived players.

As the Phillies transitioned their celebration from the pitcher's mound to the champagne-stocked locker room, Lionel decided to go with them. He spent the next several minutes in *fan heaven*, spraying champagne into the air and celebrating with his beloved heroes. He flew under the radar the entire time, except for when his buddy saw him on television in the locker room and asked, "Is that Lionel?"

While I understand some of his actions may be questionable, I actually admire his boldness and courage. Lionel wasn't content simply watching the celebration; he wanted to taste it for himself. He risked being dragged off the field by his underwear strap just so he could participate rather than watch from a distance.

Isn't it easy to feel like a spectator in life, like we're on the outside looking in? We watch our heroes live out the dreams that reside within our hearts; meanwhile, we remain firmly planted in the hard, uncomfortable bleachers.

I think we could all benefit from a little more of Lionel's mentality. How different would our lives be if we possessed the courage to put down the peanuts, squeeze our way past all the other spectators, and make our way to the field? I think we would be speechless after discovering the depth of adventure and joy waiting for us.

The difference between Lionel's story and ours is that we don't have to sneak into the action. The one who holds the oceans in the palm of His hand motions for us. He has created us to live a grand story. Our lives ooze destiny and purpose. God is inviting us to experience the life we were created to live!

But, do I really have to leave the peanuts behind? They cost five bucks and I'm thoroughly enjoying them! I have to wonder if this is what it looks like when we refuse to respond to God's call. God has a feast waiting, but we forfeit our seat at the table because we don't think we can give up the peanuts.

Isn't it challenging to give up what we can see for something yet to be seen? And yet Scripture is full of stories and scenarios where people were asked to make this very decision. Simon Peter is a good example.

INTO DEEP WATER

In the fifth chapter of Luke, Simon Peter came face to face with the question: *Is it worth it to give up what I can see for something yet to be seen?* We often zip through these stories in our daily reading plans, but if we slow down and put ourselves in Simon Peter's shoes, we can feel the weight of the decision.

I picture him standing on the shore, sweat dripping off his nose, working diligently to clean his nets. Perhaps he was in a relatively foul mood as he had just spent the night on the water without catching a single fish. Fishing was his livelihood, the way he fed his family. Was he discouraged? Frustrated? Exhausted? Did he have any idea that the Author of his story was about to flip his world upside down?

God was about to tap Peter on the shoulder. Actually, He does him one better and asks to borrow his fishing boat so He can address the massive crowd. You know the feeling, right? You're about to head out the door after a long day, and then you run into someone who needs help. Does your heart leap for joy at the opportunity to serve, or do you just want to get home to your family? Simon Peter could have offered up a few excuses, but for whatever reason, he crawled back in the boat and pushed off from shore with Jesus.

After Jesus finished addressing the crowd from the boat, He turned and made a provocative statement: *Put out into the deep water, and let down your nets for a catch* (Luke 5:4, NASB).

Deep water? Let the nets down again? I can hear the internal sigh from here. This was going to require some time and work for Simon Peter. It may have started as a cordial favor, but it was becoming evident that Jesus was after far more than a floating pulpit—He was looking for a life to invade.

I wonder what would have happened to Simon Peter if he would have said no. What if, for a variety of seemingly logical reasons, Simon Peter would have refused to set sail for deep water? Without knowing it, he would have turned down the single greatest invitation of his life.

We don't know the answer to the question because he responded in a beautiful manner. In verse five, Peter said:

Master, we worked hard all night and caught nothing, but I will do as You say and let down the nets (Luke 5:5, NASB).

Perhaps all of heaven applauded his response. His life—and the lives of countless others who would be impacted by his future ministry—were about to be forever changed because he was willing to follow Jesus into the deep.

> *When they had done so, they caught such a large number of fish that their nets began to break. So they signaled their partners in the other boat to come and help them, and they came and filled both boats so full that they began to sink.*
> (Luke 5:6-7, NIV)

Put yourself in the rickety fishing boat for a moment. Simon Peter is whooping and hollering from the sheer joy of the multitude of fish. Then, his hollering voice starts sounding a higher pitch as he realizes they're sinking. What was Jesus doing during all the excitement? We know the Creator of all things wasn't the least bit scared as water poured into the boat, so I picture Him smiling at the catch of fish. And what did He say to Simon Peter when the first tug on the nets occurred? I doubt He said, "I told you so!" Maybe He just winked.

Nonetheless, Simon Peter falls at His feet and says, "Go away from me, Lord; I am a sinful man!" Little did he know, but Jesus doesn't require us to be perfect before we agree to follow Him. The invitation has always been to come as you are. Jesus demonstrates this truth by saying, *Don't be afraid; from now on you will fish for people* (Luke 5:10, NIV).

As miraculous as the previous five minutes had been, Simon Peter still had a decision to make. Was he willing to allow Jesus to not only interrupt his day, but his entire life? What about the seven year plan he had carefully concocted? What about his dreams of a fishing show on ESPN? What about collecting on the mountain of fish he and his friends had just landed?

> *So they pulled their boats up on shore, left everything and followed him.* (Luke 5:11, NIV)

LOOSENING THE WHITE-KNUCKLED GRIP

Simon Peter successfully left the fish behind, but my three-year-old daughter, Avery, found it to be a little more difficult. Ashley and I took her to the Denver Aquarium, and while I planned on being the teacher, I ended up being the student. As soon as we walked in, Avery's eyes locked onto a small little aquarium that was located at the front entrance. The fish were small—actually tiny— but she was still fascinated by the sight of an aquarium full of bubbles and fish. I thought to myself, *If she thinks these puny little fish are cool, wait until she sees the good stuff, like the sharks!*

We stood by the small fish for a few more minutes before I started prompting Avery to move along. She wasn't budging. She had no idea what was around the corner, she just knew that what she was looking at was pretty cool. I began pleading with her, "Avery, you have to trust me on this. Follow me and I'll show you something much better."

I eventually had to pry her away from the tank, and I spent the next few moments calming her disappointment by assuring her there were much better displays ahead. Avery was struggling to leave what she could see for something yet to be seen. As her father, I knew she would enjoy the deeper water of the shark tank more than the miniature tank, but getting a three-year-old to trust you can be challenging.

In that moment I caught a glimpse of what God experiences as He invites us to follow Him around the corner and into the unknown. It's unknown to us, but it's certainly not a mystery to Him. As our Father, He understands that better things are ahead, but getting us to trust Him can also be challenging.

As humans, we typically think in terms of, *What will this cost me? What will I have to give up?* We're quite aware of what we hold in our hands, but are we ignorant of what God holds in His? We maintain a white-knuckled grip on trivial things while God urges us to let go and experience something far better.

Before we continue on the journey, I want to encourage you to stop and ponder the following questions: Are you experiencing all that God has for your life? Is there more? Are there aspects of your life where you are sitting in the stands rather than participating in the story of God? Lastly, are you willing to set sail for deeper water in your relationship with God? If so, I believe the rest of the book will be a surprising adventure for you. God has been waiting patiently for this opportunity. He is excited, and He is telling you not to be afraid.

As for Avery, she finally decided she was ready to move along. She galloped around the corner and then stopped in her tracks. Her eyes brightened and her mouth opened as she saw the sharks for the first time. As for me, I couldn't resist. I had to say it:

"I told you so."

2.
BAD IDEA?

One of my favorite family pictures is of my brother standing in nothing but a diaper as he prepared to launch himself off a ten foot diving board and into the deep water of our local swimming pool. He was only two-years-old, so he couldn't swim. You would think it was a terrible idea for multiple reasons; however, my dad was treading water below and waiting with steady and strong arms to receive the little thrill seeker.

My brother wasn't scared as he stood atop the diving board because he focused his attention on the reality of my dad rather than the danger that surrounded him. He magnified the presence of the one he trusted which resulted in a minimization of the scary circumstances. This is something we must learn to do if we are committed to following Jesus into deep water.

This is essentially the same dramatic lesson Simon Peter learned in Matthew 14. Let's pick up the story right after Jesus multiplied the two loaves of bread and five fish in order to feed thousands of people.

Immediately Jesus made the disciples get into the boat and go on ahead of him to the other side, while he dismissed the crowd. After he had dismissed them, he went up on a mountainside by himself to pray. Later that night, he was there alone, and the boat was already a considerable distance from land, buffeted by the waves because the wind was against it. (Matthew 14:22-24, NIV)

The disciples were obeying Jesus by crossing the sea. The Scriptures make it clear that it was Jesus' idea, not the disciples. By obeying Jesus and setting sail for deep water, the disciples found themselves in an extremely frightening situation.

It's important to note that when we do the same in our lives, when we truly say yes to Jesus, and when the sun sets and the shoreline disappears, we may encounter some extremely choppy water. The typical result of stepping away from what is comfortable is the arrival of feelings of discomfort. Strange, huh? But, it's in this place where we experience the life of Jesus. This is where He likes to reveal Himself.

And in the fourth watch of the night He came to them, walking on the sea. When the disciples saw Him walking on the sea, they were terrified, and said, "It is a ghost!" And they cried out in fear. But immediately Jesus spoke to them, saying, "Take courage, it is I; do not be afraid."
(Matthew 14:25-27, NASB)

What a scene—a group of manly men crying out in fear as their little boat was being pummeled by the wind and waves. They were soaking wet, clinging to whatever they could grasp to stabilize them, and crying out for God to spare their lives. They must have thought, *So, this is what happens when we obey Jesus?*

Look closely at how Jesus responded. He addressed their misunderstanding of the situation—helping them understand they weren't seeing a ghost—and then He redirected their attention to His presence, which was the key to experiencing courage. Peter, in typical fashion, was one of the first to respond.

> *Peter said to Him, "Lord, if it is You, command me to come to You on the water." And He said, "Come!" And Peter got out of the boat, and walked on the water and came toward Jesus.*
> (Matthew 14:28-29, NASB)

What a breathtaking experience! It's almost too obvious to note, but Peter would not have experienced the supernatural feeling of walking on water if he refused to step out of the boat. He (initially) magnified the reality of Jesus' presence, which allowed him to step forward in courage.

> *But seeing the wind, he became frightened, and beginning to sink, he cried out, "Lord, save me!" Immediately Jesus stretched out His hand and took hold of him, and said to him, "You of little faith, why did you doubt?"*
> (Matthew 14:30-31, NASB)

I don't want to play Monday morning quarterback here, nor do I claim to be a professional water walker, but Peter made a mistake by taking his eyes off Jesus. I'm sure it was a lesson he didn't soon dismiss.

Isn't the same true for us on a daily basis? We may not experience the gravity defying thrill of water walking, but have you ever removed your eyes from Jesus and set your gaze upon the physical circumstances that surround you? What was the result? If you're anything like me, you experienced the dismissal of peace and the arrival of fear and anxiety.

Fear can come from the enemy of our souls. The Bible gives him a name—Satan—and makes it clear that if his lips are moving, he's lying. His motive is to simply keep you on the shore. He wants to convince you that you're better off playing it *safe*. If you do set sail for deep water with Jesus, then he wants to keep you in the boat. If you do possess the courage to step out of the boat, then he wants to distract you from Jesus. He can't stop you from experiencing true life, so he has taken up the strategy of lying, deceiving, and distracting. Ultimately, he wants to convince you that following Jesus was a terrible idea.

As Christ followers, we should be aware of the tactics of the enemy. If Satan despises us because we were made in the image of God, then why would we ever listen to his lies? His desire is to "steal, kill, and destroy" (John 10:10). He wants the absolute worst for us. If he tells us to slow down, then we should speed up. If he tells us to speed up, then we should slow down. If he tells us it was a bad idea to follow Jesus, then we're right where we need to be.

THE TEMPTATION TO TURN BACK

I wouldn't be surprised if Satan tried to convince the apostle Paul that he had made a terrible mistake by yielding his life to Christ. At one time in Paul's life, he was a respected religious zealot. He had a comfortable life, and he thought he was doing God a service by arresting Christ followers.

It all changed when Jesus appeared to Paul (Saul at the time) and changed the entire course of his life, including his name. Jesus didn't tap him on the shoulder and whisper in his ear; he actually knocked him off his horse and blinded him. It wasn't exactly a polite move, but it was the best thing that could have happened to him. From a circumstantial perspective, his life was about to get a lot worse. But in the grand scheme of things, Paul was about to gain the only thing that truly matters. He would later write to the Corinthian church and explain the persecution he suffered for Christ:

Five times I received from the Jews thirty-nine lashes. Three times I was beaten with rods, once I was stoned, three times I was shipwrecked, a night and a day I have spent in the deep. I have been on frequent journeys, in dangers from rivers, dangers from robbers, dangers from my countrymen, dangers from the Gentiles, dangers in the city, dangers in the wilderness, dangers on the sea, dangers among false brethren; I have been in labor and hardship, through many sleepless nights, in hunger and thirst, often without food, in cold and exposure. Apart from such external

things, there is the daily pressure on me of concern for all the churches.
(2 Corinthians 11:24-28, NASB)

I wonder if somewhere between the fourth and fifth lashings, Paul questioned whether he had made a mistake by following Jesus—even if only a momentary thought that flashed in his mind. I'm sure the "father of all lies" (John 8) attempted to take advantage of Paul's physical circumstances by trying to convince him to stop the madness.

Despite the enemy's efforts to convince Paul to turn his back on Jesus, it didn't work. In fact, Paul made the most astounding declaration in a letter to the Philippian church:

But whatever things were gain to me, those things I have counted as loss for the sake of Christ. More than that, I count all things to be loss in view of the surpassing value of knowing Christ Jesus my Lord. (Philippians 3:7-8, NASB)

The only thing that could have possibly kept Paul from slipping into bitterness and disillusionment was a real relationship with a real Jesus. He learned to focus on the reality of Jesus more than the troubling nature of his physical circumstances. He simply wasn't willing to trade Jesus for a safer, more comfortable existence.

DID I REALLY SIGN UP FOR THIS?

Several years ago, I sensed Jesus inviting me to leave what was comfortable in order to follow Him. I had been working for a radio company in Kansas, but

Jesus was leading me to leave my full-time job (and dreams of making it big in the media industry) in order to participate in a church internship in Colorado Springs. People thought I was crazy to trade a full-time salary for an internship I would have to pay for.

Approximately fifteen months later, I found myself questioning the logic of the decision as well. I had finished the internship and was serving as an associate pastor at New Life Church, but the seas were about to turn extremely choppy.

It started with a phone call from my supervisor at the time, Bill Walton. I knew something was strange as soon as I saw his name appear on caller ID. It was 10:00 p.m., and he was calling an emergency meeting at his house.

The next few hours are hard to describe. He proceeded to tell us that some of the allegations regarding our senior pastor were actually true, and that Ted Haggard would be resigning immediately from New Life Church and from his role as president of the National Association of Evangelicals.

I had left everything to join a ministry that was seemingly now on the verge of collapsing like a homecoming bonfire. The future was uncertain to say the least. It felt as if we went from traveling down the interstate at 80 mph on a clear sunny day, to finding ourselves on a rugged mountain trail trying to navigate by nothing but moonlight.

To make matters worse, I remembered that exact week was my week to be the pastor on call, which simply meant I carried the church's cell phone and would be responsible for handling any pastoral emergencies that surfaced. I had only been a pastor for eleven months, and

I quickly felt the water levels rising around my head. *Was I really prepared for this? Did I have any idea what I was doing as a pastor? Is this really what I had signed up for?*

In reality, all of our pastors were on call that week (and in the months and years that followed). While it was very difficult, we certainly experienced the presence and faithfulness of Jesus during this troubling season. He had us firmly by the hand and provided shelter from the storm. I would compare it to a father who grabs hold of his child's hand just before crossing a busy intersection. Sure, it may be a dangerous situation, but there is a sense of security and comfort because of the one leading the way.

Someone asked me recently if I would agree to do it all again if I actually knew what was coming. I didn't even have to think about it. "Absolutely," I responded. In that season, I gained a deeper understanding of who Jesus really is. I came to know His love for me and His love for people in a way I didn't understand before. I was reminded that no matter how uncertain life's circumstances may be, God's steadfast faithfulness will remain.

It's interesting that Jesus not only invites us to follow Him into deeper water, but He actually gives us a weather forecast as well. We shouldn't be surprised when the winds pick up and the waves seem daunting.

In fact, in some of Paul's final words, he writes to Timothy and explains that *everyone who wants to live a godly life in Christ Jesus will suffer persecution* (2 Timothy 3:12, NLT). He was probably tipped off by Jesus' words on the same topic: *Here on earth you will have many trials and sorrows. But take heart, because I have overcome the world* (John 16:33, NLT).

Jesus never said it would be a Sunday stroll in the park. However, if life's path didn't twist and turn and disappear around the bend, we wouldn't need a guide. If we didn't need a guide, we would miss our greatest gift in life—knowing the guide.

3.
BECOMING OLD FRIENDS

There was a time in my life when I was convinced I would never allow sushi to touch my lips. To be honest, I didn't even know what sushi was until five or six years ago. I was utterly perplexed when I discovered that people actually paid money in order to consume raw fish. It sounded more like an appropriate method of extracting information from terrorists than the centerpiece of a romantic meal.

Bear in mind that I grew up in western Kansas, a place where beef is king. I am—and always will be—a proud carnivore. This is why I cringed when another couple recently invited my wife, Ashley, and I on a double date to a local sushi restaurant. Their company would be very enjoyable, but I was prepared for the food to be hard to swallow.

From the moment we walked in the front door, my buddy, John, began raving about how delicious the food would be. He said, "Gabe, this food will melt in your mouth. Once you actually taste it, you'll be hooked for life." While his passion for sushi created a mild level of curiosity, I still had no real interest in allowing raw fish to come anywhere near my taste buds.

My plan was to take small bites and not think about what I was eating. With this in mind, I cut off my first piece and slowly lifted it to my mouth—trying hard to avoid using a majority of my senses. It wasn't what I thought it would be. Not only was it bearable, but it was quite good. I looked across the table and said, "This is surprisingly delicious!"

Tasting sushi goodness required me to get past my preconceived ideas and actually experience it for myself. The reality of sushi was very different than the expectation that I had concocted in my head. If it weren't for John's persistent invitation, I would have missed out on goodness I never knew existed. I think the same is required in order to experience the goodness of Jesus. We have to lay aside all of the things we've heard or thought about Him and actually experience Him for ourselves. We have to "taste and see that the Lord is good" (Psalm 34:8).

When I was a kid, I thought Jesus was kind of spooky. The image I had of Him was partially formed by different pictures that adorned the church walls. He was ghostly looking, extremely pale, and He stared off into space. He looked disconnected and disengaged. There were other pictures that painted Him as a small, dainty man wandering around with sheep. Honestly, He looked fairly miserable. He certainly wasn't anyone I was interested in getting to know.

And yet, I also sensed an invitation. In a hard to explain way, I felt like I was being beckoned. I guess you could say I heard the knocking.

Jesus said, Look! I stand at the door and knock. If you hear my voice and open the door, I will come in, and we will share a meal together as friends. (Revelation 3:20, NLT)

Share a meal with Mr. Miserable? I think I would have rather eaten raw fish . . . alone. While I heard Him knocking, I wasn't about to open the door. I ignored Him as if He were standing on my front porch trying to sell me a set of kitchen knives or an overpriced vacuum cleaner.

My ignorance and hard-heartedness didn't deter Him. I eventually opened the door and realized there weren't any kitchen knives in His hands (though oddly enough, it was evident He had been pierced by something sharp).

The holes in His hands and feet are evidence that Jesus has gone through extraordinary measures to be known—to make God known. The Creator of all things became flesh and endured the brutality of Roman crucifixion so He could call us friends. This was His intent all along.

God has always wanted to enjoy communion with His people. The same mouth that spoke the galaxies into existence breathed life into Adam and Eve; then He walked and talked with them in the cool of the day. They enjoyed each other's company. They were friends. While Adam and Eve betrayed God's friendship in the Garden, Jesus restored all that was lost by submitting to the cross.

After Jesus was resurrected, we see Him doing something that came so naturally to Him—He was enjoying His friendships.

The twenty-first chapter of John paints a rich picture of Jesus and friendship. Peter and a few of the other disciples had just spent the night fishing under the stars. What they didn't know is that they were about to be surprised by the very one who hung those stars in place.

Early in the morning, Jesus stood on the shore, but the disciples did not realize that it was Jesus. He called out to them, "Friends, haven't you any fish?"

"No," they answered.

He said, "Throw your net on the right side of the boat and you will find some." When they did, they were unable to haul the net in because of the large number of fish.

Then the disciple whom Jesus loved said to Peter, "It is the Lord!" As soon as Simon Peter heard him say, "It is the Lord," he wrapped his outer garment around him (for he had taken it off) and jumped into the water. The other disciples followed in the boat, towing the net full of fish, for they were not far from shore, about a hundred yards. When they landed, they saw a fire of burning coals there with fish on it, and some bread.

Jesus said to them, "Bring some of the fish you have just caught." So Simon Peter climbed back into the boat and dragged the net ashore. It was full of large fish, 153, but even with so many the net was not torn. Jesus said to them, "Come and have breakfast." None of the disciples dared ask him, "Who are you?" They knew it was the Lord. Jesus came, took the bread and gave it to them, and did the same with the fish. This was now the third time Jesus appeared to his disciples after he was raised from the dead. (John 21:4-14, NIV)

This is exactly the kind of God I want to know. Jesus desired nothing more than to sit around the campfire and enjoy breakfast with His friends. Can you imagine if you were granted a log around that campfire? What would it have been like to drink in that experience? Just how large were their smiles? The roar of laughter erupting over the cracks and pops of the fire. Tears welling up in the disciples' eyes as they realized their friend was back. Peter rehashing his *walking on the water* story. Jesus reminding Peter that it smelled like skunk every time he fished without Jesus. More laughter. More tears.

Jesus was with His friends, and I believe His heart was overflowing with joy. My heart overflows at the mere thought of calling that same Jesus a friend. It surpasses anything in my current vernacular. The Scriptures state that Jesus is the same "yesterday, today, and forever" (Hebrews 13:8). We can know Jesus just like the disciples did. We're invited into the story and granted the same access.

Actually, we can know Him better than the disciples did. Jesus Himself said that it was better if He went away, because then He would send the Holy Spirit (John 16:7). The Spirit of Christ not only walks beside us, He actually resides within us. What could be better than that?

Pause for a few moments and let the weight of this truth settle on your heart: God lives in you. That automatically puts Him in a more intimate category than any other friend. He's closer than the air you breathe. The same Spirit that hovered over the waters at creation in Genesis 1 has chosen to take up residence in you.

So, what exactly is He doing now that He lives in you?

I can assure you that He's not sleeping. The Bible states that you are a temple in which He lives, not a cave in which He hibernates. He's vibrant. He's lively. He wants to engage you in deep relationship. He wants to speak to you.

An important element of being a Christ follower is learning to recognize His voice. This is not a special privilege afforded to a select few, but this is the foundation for Christian living. Jesus said, *The gatekeeper opens the gate for him, and the sheep listen to his voice. He calls his own sheep by name and leads them out. When he has brought out all his own, he goes on ahead of them, and his sheep follow him because they know his voice* (John 10:3-4, NLT).

If you have said *yes* to following Jesus, you have been given the distinct privilege of being numbered among the sheep. While that may not sound enticing—sheep aren't the smartest creatures—it's actually an amazing opportunity. Now you get to hear from Him; you get to know the Shepherd and Guide on a personal basis—and He's much more intriguing than the pictures portray.

In fact, I've found Him to be compelling, engaging, funny, kind, strong, gentle, brilliant, fierce, and safe. He's nothing like I once imagined.

WILL GOD SPEAK TO YOU?

One of the most common statements I hear in ministry and counseling sessions is: *I believe God speaks, I just don't think I'll be able to hear Him.* This statement is saturated with the lies of the enemy. Satan works hard at trying to convince you that you'll be left out, that there is something wrong with you that will inhibit you from personally hearing from God.

I've also had the privilege of walking along with several of these same people as they discovered the truth—that God was indeed speaking to them personally, and He had a lot to say. I remember looking into the tear-filled eyes of a ten-year-old as he said: "I finally heard God speak to me. I always thought He would speak to my family, but I never thought He would actually speak to me."

I've sat with many others who were, by their own candid admission, living pretty messed up lives. They were far from perfect. They also learned that hearing from Jesus didn't depend upon their behavior, but rather on their position as sons and daughters of an extremely relational God. This is so important to understand, because Jesus is ready and willing to communicate with you at this very moment. He's not waiting for you to get everything in order before He'll speak. His words are needed now—right where you are-- because they provide the heart change that leads to the behavior change.

God reminded me of this truth on the very first day of my counseling practicum. I was a fish out of water with no real counseling experience. My first appointment was with a person who was dealing with some very serious mental disorders, and had just been released from prison for stabbing someone. My first thought was, *I have no idea what I'm doing, God . . . help!*

As I drove to the clinic, I heard God whisper the following to my heart: *Gabe, it's my words spoken to someone's heart that create real life change.* Counseling techniques and skills are useful, but God was commissioning me to listen to Him and teach others to do the same.

The next several months were filled with stories of people discovering hope because they discovered friendship with Jesus. Their tangled lives started to become less tangled as they started listening with different ears. It didn't happen overnight, but it was a journey several were willing to embark upon.

Eventually, I heard many of the same questions surface: "How do I know it's really Him?" and "How can I tell the difference between His voice and my own thoughts?" These are good questions. I've asked them, too—especially when I've sensed God ask me to do something difficult.

Before I married Ashley, I had the daunting task of saving enough money to buy a diamond. I didn't make a lot of money, so I knew it would require some sort of divine intervention. I remember the giddy feeling in the pit of my stomach when I finally realized I had enough money in the bank to start ring shopping. I also remember how the giddiness turned to knots as I heard Jesus speak to my heart: *What if you give this money to John*?

What? John is not a pretty little blonde with whom I desired to spend the rest of my life. He is a six feet four inch, 275-pound mountain of a man—a man who was also trying to scrape together enough money to buy his soon-to-be wife a diamond. God was simply asking me to help a brother out. I tried valiantly to convince myself that I was making it all up: *This must be my own thoughts. I didn't hear from God. Maybe I just ate bad pizza for lunch.*

I couldn't escape the truth, because I knew I had heard from God. How did I know? I recognized His voice. Remember Jesus' words from John 10: "the sheep follow Him because they know His voice." I had the choice to acknowledge His voice and follow Him or blow it all off as a figment of my imagination.

God saw the mental wrestling match unfolding between my ears, and He decided to intervene. His next statement was clear and concise: *If you want my best, you'll trust me.*

Checkmate. I couldn't do any more mental gymnastics to avoid the truth. I was ready to trust the words of my friend, Jesus, and follow His lead. Plus, I was intrigued by what He had in store. He was up to something special, and I wasn't about to miss out.

My phone rang a few days later. The man on the other end—who I had only met one time—started by saying: "Gabe, this may sound strange to you . . . but I had a thought pop into my head a few days ago, and I think it was from God." I could hear a hint of excitement in his voice as he said, "I want to send you a check so you can buy an engagement ring for your girlfriend."

My face was invaded by a giant smile. I thought to myself, *That was impressive, God*. The man on the phone had no idea that I had any intention of proposing to my girlfriend, that is, unless he was tipped off as part of a divine conspiracy.

I started high-stepping around the living room in joyous celebration as I opened the check. The amount was much higher than expected. After I purchased the ring,

I heard the familiar voice of Jesus, again: *Let this be a continual reminder that I will always provide for you.*

What a friend.

RECOGNIZING HIS VOICE

Hearing from Jesus has been the single greatest contributor to the joy I've experienced in life. I never knew how deeply kind and generous He was until I demonstrated a willingness to taste and see for myself. Getting to know Him has been a process requiring commitment, intentionality, and time. It's basically what's required of all healthy relationships.

I've also had moments of frustration. There have been times when I haven't necessarily heard Him correctly. I thought He was telling me one thing, but it turned out to be something else. I think this is common in the process of spiritual growth, especially considering there are multiple voices at play—my own ideas, the voice of the enemy, the voice of other people, and so on. We have to be committed to tuning and retuning our ears to the voice of Jesus. We do this by filling our hearts and minds with truth from Scripture.

I believe one of the best ways to learn to recognize the voice of Jesus is by memorizing Bible verses. Ask God to show you a new verse or passage to memorize each week. When my relationship with God was in its infancy, He would often speak to me by simply reminding me of different verses I had previously memorized. The more time I spent in the Scriptures, the more God was training my spiritual ears to hear Him. Simply put, hearing from Jesus is often a matter of discerning truth. Jesus is truth

(John 14:6). He'll never speak anything that contradicts the truth of Scripture, although He may speak something that conflicts with your understanding of Scripture. (Just ask the Pharisees!)

Neither is Jesus in the business of condemning you. Paul writes, *Therefore there is now no condemnation for those who are in Christ Jesus* (Romans 8:1, NASB). In your time of listening, be aware of anything that resembles condemnation: *You'll never figure this out. You don't have what it takes. You always come up short. God doesn't want to speak to you.* There is certainly an accuser, but he's the Antichrist—the opposite of all that is true about God. Jesus' words are designed to strengthen, encourage, and comfort. They produce the fruit of the Spirit: love, joy, peace, patience, kindness, goodness, faithfulness, gentleness, and self-control (Galatians 5:22-23).

Finally, try not to complicate the matter. Remind yourself of the basics: God created you for relationship. His love for you cannot be measured. He wants to be known. He desires intimacy.

With a renewed mind, engage Him in an authentic manner. Ask Him legitimate questions. Talk to Him as a friend. Listen to Him as a friend. Then wake up the next day and do it all again. After all, as the saying goes, "It takes a long time to become old friends."

4.

TYPICAL DAY: RADICAL OBEDIENCE

Listening to Jesus is the easy part; obeying His words is much more difficult.

Can you relate? Do you have a story similar to my ring story; a time when you wrestled with whether you actually wanted to obey what God was saying? You can remain pretty comfortable in the process of listening, but obedience often requires a popping of our comfort bubble.

A strange thing happens as we live out our lives on planet Earth. Somewhere along the way we develop comfort zones, and we assume our lives are safest within these zones. It feels safe and comfortable because it's familiar; it's what we are used to. When we are familiar with a situation or circumstance, we often feel like we're in control. When we feel like we're in control, we tend to ignore God and depend upon our own wisdom, strength, and resources. God slowly gets edged out of the equation.

This is not a safe place to reside—it's actually quite dangerous. We have a very real enemy who desires to "kill, steal, and destroy" (John 10:10). Peter urges us:

Stay alert! Watch out for your great enemy, the devil. He prowls around like a roaring lion, looking for someone to devour (1 Peter 5:8, NLT). Notice the enemy is actively looking for someone to devour. He's hunting his prey, and the easiest prey are those who are comfortably living life on their own terms; those who have no interest in listening to or obeying Jesus.

Like any good hunter, the enemy wants to remain concealed. He doesn't want us to be aware of the danger that may lurk around the corner. He wants us to be ignorant of the spiritual battle that surrounds us. Paul writes: *For we are not fighting against flesh-and-blood enemies, but against evil rulers and authorities of the unseen world, against mighty powers in this dark world, and against evil spirits in the heavenly places* (Ephesians 6:12, NLT). If you're breathing, the enemy has marked you as a target. Have you ever considered the notion that your life is opposed? Perhaps this will help you see things from a different perspective. You are despised by Satan because you are cherished by God. Your life is designed to bring God glory, so the enemy wants to thwart you at every turn. At the same time, we shouldn't be afraid because *greater is He who is in us than he who is in the world* (1 John 4:4, NASB).

Because the spiritual battle is real, it's crucial that we learn to obey Jesus. We can't see the whole picture, so we must rely on the one who can. His words are designed to lead and guide us into safe pasture and quiet waters (Psalm 23). We tend to listen best when we're aware that the waters aren't calm; when life seems the most unsure. This was the case on my first rafting trip down the Arkansas River.

It was the summer of my seventh grade year, and I weighed all of about eighty pounds. My parents approached me one day with what they thought was an exciting announcement: "We're going to go white water rafting through the Royal Gorge this summer!"

I think I turned as pale as the Jesus pictures. My mind instantly came up with a scenario that had me being ejected from the raft in the middle of the rapids and being swept away for good. I spent the next few months wondering if I would survive the trip. The rafting adventure approached like a funnel cloud in tornado alley (you see it coming, so you prepare yourself for impact).

My preparation included lifting weights. I thought I could maybe bulk up to eighty-five pounds over the few months before the trip and develop the strength to paddle the Class 4 rapids. Fat chance! My feeble and prepubescent arms would be no match for the raging river, no matter how many times I bench-pressed the empty bar.

Our guide, it turned out, looked like he could handle it. He was a football player at Colorado State University who spent his summers leading people down this furious death trap of a river. His arms were chiseled, but most importantly, he appeared confident. He assured us he had been down the river countless times. Wearing a commanding expression, he boomed: "It's crucial that you do exactly what I tell you to do when I tell you to do it."

He went on to explain: "We are going to encounter some serious rapids, including Sunshine Falls." I zoned out after hearing the word, "falls." I'm glad my parents didn't tell me in advance that we would be rafting over a waterfall. My nerves were running higher than the 1,200 foot towering cliffs that outlined the river. It was a simple reminder that there was no way out.

We practiced following orders on the calm water as our beloved drill sergeant yelled: "Right, Right, Right! Now, back-paddle. Harder. HARDER!" We passed the test, but I wondered if he was slightly nervous about his lightweight passenger. I think I saw him straining extra hard on his oars as he realized I wasn't much help.

I was bounced around like a pinball on the first few rapids. Not only was I zero help in steering the raft, but my dad had trouble rowing because he was too busy trying to keep me safe. He did his best to clinch the back of my life vest and still row, but the guide decided it would be better for me to abort my oar and move to the center of the raft. My new job description was simple: Hold on for dear life.

We approached Sunshine Falls and pulled our raft to the side of the river. The guide wanted us to get out and survey our route before we continued. My seventh grade imagination was happy to see that the falls didn't resemble the waterfalls I had pictured (namely Niagara), but it was still plenty scary. I could barely hear myself think over the roar of the rushing water, but I leaned in to hear what the guide was saying. I looked around to see the same attentive stare from everyone. We were hanging on his every word. This was not the place for distraction or disobedience.

After viewing the chosen route, we got back into the raft and approached the series of dangerous rapids. The guide still sounded confident, but the pace and intensity of his orders increased significantly. I was hunkered down and hanging on to a rope attached to the center of the raft. As we hit the rapids, my arms were stretched back and forth like a rubber band. The rest of the team paddled mightily as they followed the exact orders of the guide: "Right, hard! Now left . . . back . . . two forward!" They didn't understand the reason for all of the commands, but nobody was about to argue.

We smiled in relief after we made it through the unmerciful falls. I've never witnessed a situation where a group of grown adults were so ready to follow orders from a vacationing college kid. Thankfully, they did. He knew precisely what he was doing the entire time.

Dangerous and precarious situations have a way of funneling our attention and inspiring our obedience. It is easy to follow orders when your life is on the line.

What would it take to possess this same commitment to obedience on a typical day? I think this is exactly what Jesus is looking for. We may not feel like we're in great danger as we pack our lunch, hug our kids, and drive to the office, but does that mean we are free from the wiles and tactics of the enemy? Does that mean we should take the day off from listening to and obeying Jesus?

Our comfort zone doesn't provide a magical covering where the enemy will stop attempting to steal our joy, oppose our marriages, destroy our families, wreck our finances, and rob our health. Just because we feel like it's a typical day doesn't mean we can go to sleep spiritually. We must remain alert and possess a willingness to readily respond to the words of Jesus. We must learn to abide in His words. (Yes, even on Monday!)

Jesus emphasized this point in John 15. It was the night He would be arrested, brutally beaten, and hauled away to face His eventual crucifixion. The disciples didn't see it coming, but Jesus worked hard to prepare them for the inevitable truth.

> *Yes, I am the vine; you are the branches. Those who remain in me, and I in them, will produce much fruit. For apart from me you can do nothing. Anyone who does not remain in me is thrown away like a useless branch and withers. Such branches are gathered into a pile to be burned. But if you remain in me and my words remain in you, you may ask for anything you want, and it will be granted! When you produce much fruit, you are my true disciples. This brings great glory to my Father.*
>
> *I have loved you even as the Father has loved me. Remain in my love. When you obey my commandments, you remain in my love, just as I obey my Father's commandments and remain in his love.* (John 15:5-10, NLT)

In these, some of His final words before death, Jesus is driving home the importance of obedience. I'm not sure if the disciples afforded Him the same attentive stare we gave our rafting guide on the verge of the falls, but the situation certainly called for it. In no time at all, Jesus would be gone and the flock would be scattered. Jesus commanded them to remain obedient to His words.

Not only does obedience bring protection, but it produces amazing results—fruit. When God speaks, things happen. His words create. All that can be seen and all that is unseen is a result of the spoken words of God. God said, "Let there be light," and it happened. The far reaches of the universe came into being because of the indescribable power exerted through His words. There is nothing more powerful.

> *The voice of the LORD echoes above the sea.*
> *The God of glory thunders.*
> *The LORD thunders over the mighty sea.*
> *The voice of the LORD is powerful;*
> * the voice of the LORD is majestic.*
> *The voice of the LORD splits the mighty cedars;*
> * the LORD shatters the cedars of Lebanon.*
> *He makes Lebanon's mountains skip like a calf;*
> * he makes Mount Hermon leap like a young wild ox.*
> *The voice of the LORD strikes*
> * with bolts of lightning.*
> *The voice of the LORD makes the barren wilderness quake;*
> * the LORD shakes the wilderness of Kadesh.*
> *The voice of the LORD twists mighty oaks*
> * and strips the forests bare.*
> *In his Temple everyone shouts, "Glory!"*
> (Psalm 29:3-9, NLT)

His words can't be slowed, maimed, or detoured. They are unstoppable. Knowing this, who would want to stand opposed to what He has spoken? A feather would have a better chance of stopping a freight train than anything in this world stopping the Word of God. This is precisely why it's wise to find out what He has spoken (and is speaking) and remain in alignment with that power. I guess you could say it's kind of like surfing.

REMAINING IN ALIGNMENT WITH GOD

By the way, I did eventually learn to actually stay on the board and experience the *exhilarating* feeling of surfing. It was everything I hoped it would be, once I figured it out. The power of the ocean beneath my feet was truly unforgettable. In order to experience this awesome adventure, I had to understand the importance of cooperating with the ocean.

My responsibility was to locate the waves, position myself on the board, wait for the right timing, paddle like crazy, and eventually pop up and enjoy the ride. The ocean's responsibility was to provide the power and momentum to make it all possible.

In the same way, God's words provide the power and momentum necessary to produce fruit in our lives and in our world. They're the unstoppable wave. Our responsibility is to locate the wave by understanding what He's speaking and remain in alignment (agreement) with it through obedience. The result will be the exhilarating feeling of moving in step with the one who has power over all things.

I sat with a couple of good friends recently and listened to them each describe discouraging marital situations. They took turns talking about all that was wrong with their marriages, and both men admitted they were on the brink of divorce. I was surprised to hear these words coming from their mouths. They were both men who loved God.

After a long period of listening, I finally spoke up and asked a simple question: *What is God speaking over your marriages?*

Their heads turned simultaneously, and I could see the curiosity building as they asked me to explain. "Think about it," I continued, "The Scriptures state that 'No word of God will ever fail' (Luke 1:37), so one of the most powerful and healthy things you can do for your marriage is to find out what God is speaking and remain in agreement with it."

I went on to talk about the encounters Zacharias and Mary each had with the angel Gabriel as he delivered a word from God. After Zacharias doubted the message, Gabriel responded, *And behold, you shall be silent and unable to speak until the day when these things take place, because you did not believe my words, which will be fulfilled in their proper time* (Luke 1:20, NASB).

Every word from God will indeed be fulfilled in its proper time. In this case, the angel thought it necessary for Zacharias to be mute. That was an interesting twist to the story. I think one of the reasons he lost his ability to talk was to ensure he wouldn't speak out in unbelief, thus removing himself from alignment with God's *wave*.

One of the guys looked at me, and with deep conviction in his voice, admitted, "My marriage would be a lot better if I couldn't speak."

Mary, on the other hand, believed the message of God would be fulfilled. She responded by saying, "May it be done to me according to your word." She fully yielded to what God had spoken regarding her life, and her faith kept her in alignment with His plans.

I went on to encourage my friends to ask God to reveal what He was speaking over their marriages. Then I challenged them to believe the word, pray the word, walk in obedience to the word, and patiently wait for the fulfillment of what was promised. "If you remain in alignment," I said with a smile, "you'll see God working in mighty ways." Finally, I reminded them of what was written in Isaiah 55:

> For as the rain and the snow come down from heaven,
> And do not return there without watering the earth
> And making it bear and sprout,
> And furnishing seed to the sower and bread to the eater;
> So will My word be which goes forth from My mouth;
> It will not return to Me empty,
> Without accomplishing what I desire,
> And without succeeding in the matter for which I sent it.
> (Isaiah 55:10-11, NASB)

Soon after, I decided to take my own advice. I asked God what He was speaking over my marriage. He responded by giving me two words: *patience* and *proactivity*. I knew where He was going right away. He was looking for me to be more patient with Ashley, to seek to understand before I'm understood. I also knew what He was saying in regard to being proactive. Ashley's love language is "acts of service." Scrubbing the kitchen floor is worth more than two dozen roses in her book. God was gently telling me to be more proactive in how I served my bride.

I sat back and began pondering what I could do around the house. He interrupted my thoughts and said . . .

Start with the toilets.

Exhilarating.

"WHAT'S HE SPEAKING TODAY?"

It's amazing how much we'll see God's faithfulness when we remain in agreement with His words. Pause and take some time to ask God what He's speaking over your life. What aspects of your life are a cause for concern? What is God saying? What is He speaking over your job? Your spouse? Children? Finances? Stay with the questions until you hear answers. Then allow His words to marinate in your heart. Renew your mind and remind yourself often of what you heard. Most importantly, possess a radical commitment to obey . . . even on a typical day.

SECTION II
THE DEEP WATER OF
THE FATHER'S HEART

And may you have the power to understand, as all God's people should, how wide, how long, how high, and how deep his love is. (Ephesians 3:17, NLT)

5.

THROUGH HIS EYES

God doesn't flaunt His power like a teenaged lifeguard, blowing His whistle and issuing commands just because He can; He's strictly motivated by His great love for you. There's a specific purpose to every word and command, and the purpose is love. Because He loves you, He wants the absolute best for you. He'll settle for nothing less.

Remember Jesus' words from John 15: *When you obey my commandments, you remain in my love, just as I obey my Father's commandments and remain in his love* (John 15:10, NLT).

The words of Jesus are designed to propel us deeper into the reality of God's love. That's exactly where He's leading us. He wants us to experience the depth, width, height, and length of God's immeasurable love (Ephesians 3:17-18). Isn't it easier to obey when we understand this truth?

Jesus wants you to experience the same love He experienced. This love originates in the heart of the Heavenly Father. Essentially, Jesus is leading you into the deep water of the Father's heart, a place He knew well. Everything Jesus ever did or said was designed to teach us about the true nature of the Father. He said, *Truly, truly, I say to you, the Son can do nothing of Himself, unless it is something He sees the Father doing; for whatever the Father does, these things the Son also does in like manner. For the Father loves the Son, and shows Him all things that He Himself is doing . . .* (John 5:19-20, NASB) Jesus also said: *All things have been handed over to Me by My Father; and no one knows the Son except the Father; nor does anyone know the Father except the Son, and anyone to whom the Son wills to reveal Him* (Matthew 11:27, NASB). The Son is in the business of revealing the Father. The Jesus we see in the Scriptures is an exact representation of the Father. He carried His heart and enjoyed His love.

The problem is that people often try and separate the two. The Pharisees wanted the Father without the Son. Jesus passionately declared to their deaf ears: *If God were your Father, you would love me, because I have come to you from God. I am not here on my own, but he sent me. Why can't you understand what I am saying? It's because you can't even hear me!* (John 8:42-43, NLT).

Others want the Son without the Father. Ashley and I listened to a good friend recently admit that she felt like God the Father was creepy. "I'm ok with Jesus," she said, "but I struggle with God as a Father." It wasn't a mystery how our friend had arrived at this place of stiff-arming the Father; she grew up living under the roof of an angry and distant dad, and she found herself projecting this image onto God.

She understood on a cognitive level that God wasn't creepy, but something within her cringed at the thought of embracing her Heavenly Father. All the while, I could sense God's heartbreak over His daughter's misunderstanding.

I sat across the table and began to think about what it would be like for me if Avery and Sophie thought I was creepy. It would pierce the core of my being. I encouraged my friend to ask God an honest question: *"What's it like for you, God, to watch me keep you at bay? How does it affect you when I hold onto the belief that you are creepy as a Father?"*

My friend isn't alone. I've sat with many men and women who were struggling to understand God as Father because they had experienced earthly fathers who were all in the running for the *worst father ever* prize. (Is there a mug for that?) I've seen countless tears flow as people recounted stories of abuse and neglect from their father, the person they should have been able to trust the most. It's tragic. I would only last about three days in the counseling profession if stories ended there. It would be far too depressing. The reason I'm energized by counseling is because I've seen hope rise in people's souls as they discover that their Heavenly Father is much different. Jesus put it this way:

Or what man is there among you who, when his son asks for a loaf, will give him a stone? Or if he asks for a fish, he will not give him a snake, will he? If you then, being evil, know how to give good gifts to your children, how much more will your Father who is in heaven give what is good to those who ask Him! (Matthew 7:9-11, NASB)

Jesus referenced parents who were giving good gifts to their children. We can assume that they must have been fairly good parents by human standards. Jesus called them "evil." I think He was trying to make His point perfectly clear: The Heavenly Father is in a completely different league than even the best parents on earth. He can't be compared. There is nothing evil about your Heavenly Father. There is nothing dark in Him. He is love and He is light.

Others haven't experience an abusive father, but perhaps a father that was disconnected emotionally. I listened as another person recently said, "I don't think much about God as a Father. I guess it might be a result of having a father who wasn't very engaged in my life." She paused momentarily to ensure the floodgates holding back the tears didn't burst, and then continued, "My dad always provided for me, and he said he was proud of me on a couple occasions, but he's always been distant." She paused again, wearing the sting of the pain on her face, and then said, "I guess I've always assumed the Heavenly Father was the same."

That's a costly assumption to harbor. It surely cost her the joy of experiencing the Father's love, delight, and affection. Fortunately, it's not too late for her to start experiencing it. Neither is it too late for Brian to experience the true nature of his Heavenly Father. Brian recently admitted to me that he only felt his dad's love after he had achieved something. The result was that he felt like he had to earn his Heavenly Father's love, too. Like a dog chasing its tail, he wasted his efforts in pursuit of something he already possessed. If only he would have understood the Father's true nature years ago. It would have saved him a lot of anxiety.

Discovering the true Father requires a willingness to recognize that we may currently hold assumptions about the Father that aren't true. Some are obvious, but others might lie hidden in our hearts and minds.

Do you think this is true with you? If so, ask God to reveal these misbeliefs and assumptions in your picture of God. Then ask Him to erase the picture and replace it with a more accurate one of Himself. This will be a process that requires time, but it's an extremely rich experience. I've found that a good starting place is by beginning to look at life from the Father's perspective, by taking a look through His eyes.

BECOMING A FATHER

Before Avery was born, I had several guys tell me that I would never be the same after my first child was born. They explained that there is something that happens in a man's heart the moment he gets to hold his child for the first time. I found this to be true. It's hard to explain, but it is so true.

I think I was very prepared for the actual birthing process. Ashley and I had spent the previous three months in strict training as we participated in a birthing class. Week after week we showed up to practice breathing techniques. The men in our class all carried the same look: *Glad I'm not the one who has to push this baby out.* Without confirming it with one another, I think Bill Cosby's words were in the forefront of all of our minds: "If a man is wondering what it's like to have a baby, he should just grab his bottom lip and pull it right over the top of his head!"

This mental picture made me all the happier to have my role instead of Ashley's. After the marathon series of classes ended, I felt as confident as ever to fulfill my delivery responsibilities.

The due date came and passed without much happening. A few days later, Ashley woke up feeling sick and was experiencing abnormal pain in her side. We decided to take her to the doctor to find out if everything was OK. After an ultrasound, the doctor made the decision to induce. That was a wild moment. It dawned on me that I was going to be a dad within twenty-four hours. It was time to use those breathing skills I had worked so hard to perfect.

The next few hours were a blur, so I'll fast forward to 11 p.m. Ashley was confined to a rock hard hospital bed, huffing and puffing. I was a focused man. I took a few deep breaths and began doing what I was trained to do. Every eight seconds I told her she looked beautiful, reminded her to relax her eyebrows, and held her right leg in the air.

As prepared as I thought I was, in the heat of battle, I couldn't remember a few of the minor details. *Was it hee-hawww-whoooo or whooo-heee-hawww?* My mind struggled to recall, so I just resorted to telling her how beautiful she was. It's hard for a man to go wrong by reminding his wife of this truth. I sensed that Ashley would receive pleasure hearing this at a time when she felt like a marshmallow, while also trying to pass a bowling ball through a straw.

After a couple hours of continued labor, I saw a sight that will forever be etched in my memory. I saw the top of Avery's head. I got so excited that Ashley had to shush me. After all my elite training, I was losing focus. I was blowing it. The sheer excitement of seeing the baby crown was throwing me off. Ashley's rebuke forced me to get my head back in the game, and once again, I went back to telling her to relax her eyebrows and breathe.

Ashley did a phenomenal job delivering Avery. She was born at 3:41 a.m. After she was born, we quickly placed her on Ashley's chest and they shared an incredibly powerful momma-daughter moment. Ashley grew up dreaming about this moment. She had always wanted to be a momma. She never had big dreams to appear on the cover of magazines, build a successful business empire, or take the world by storm; she just wanted to have kids and love them well. In that moment, her dream became a reality, and she looked great in her new role.

At about 6:30 a.m. the three of us were squeezed into a tiny hospital bed, enjoying time together as a new family. A nurse entered the room, scooped Avery up, commented on her color, and quickly left the room. That was a little unnerving. Apparently, Avery's lips were abnormally purple, so they decided to rush her into the NICU. I had already been through a roller coaster of emotions, and now the story was taking a horrible turn in the wrong direction.

I still feel a twinge of pain in my heart as I remember seeing Avery for the first time, through a glass window, hooked up to all those different machines. I entered the room, leaned down next to her sweet little ears, and whispered, "Avery, it's daddy." A faint smile appeared on her face. My heart melted. I was confident that she recognized my voice. From the time we found out we were expecting Avery, we were intentional about talking to her. We sang to her, prayed for her, and affirmed our great love for her while she was in the womb. To this day, I am still convinced that she recognized her dad's voice in the midst of the beeping and buzzing of the medical instruments that surrounded her.

Avery's story didn't abruptly end in the NICU. God's grace was apparent as she began to show immediate improvement. Her lungs eventually adjusted to breathing the fresh, but thin, Colorado air and they transferred her back to our room. In a matter of two days, we were back in the comfort of our own home, starting family life as a tribe of three.

I noticed something shift in my heart in the days that followed. It was as if my heart became enlarged and I possessed a greater capacity to love this little individual. I smiled as I recalled the words of my friends, and I said to myself: *They were right. I'll never be the same.*

The only smile larger than mine was the smile I sensed God possess as He watched me *get it*. I think He was delighted that I was viewing life from a different perspective—the perspective of a father. I looked into the eyes of my daughter and told her I would do anything in the world for her, even lay down my own life. Hearing those words leave my mouth reminded me that my Father in heaven felt the same way about me. It gave me a fresh appreciation for the events that unfolded at Calvary.

THE FATHER'S LOVE IS PERSONAL

Have you spent much time considering the gospel from the Father's perspective? When I think about the remarkable wonder of the gospel, I usually think of Jesus. What would it have been like to be stripped naked, blindfolded, beaten mercilessly, spit upon, lashed, pierced, and nailed to a cross? My heart stands amazed at the courage, love, and sacrifice He displayed. My wonder and worship deepen as I consider the same event through the Father's eyes. What would it have been like for the Father to watch His Son experience the torture? How painful was that for the Father? The scene from Mel Gibson's movie, *Passion of the Christ*, depicts a teardrop that falls from heaven as Jesus died. It was a powerful addition to an already gripping scene, because it captured the heartache the Father surely experienced. I think most parents would rather experience pain themselves than watch their children suffer.

What does this tell us about the Father? Just how deep is His love? It gives a fresh perspective to one of the most famous verses in the Bible: *For God so loved the world, that He gave His only begotten Son, that whoever believes in Him shall not perish, but have eternal life* (John 3:16, NASB).

This is where it gets really personal. The Father endured the pain of watching His only Son suffer because He loves you. The Son suffered so you could know the matchless love of the Father.

This is the wonder of the Father's love.

This is the wonder of the gospel.

6.
BEAR HUG

If you wear pink or light blue to the Jenkins' home, you'll end up being camouflaged in a sea of girl toys. My head sank deeper in the pink and blue waters last Christmas as the girls opened their presents. (Sophie is our second daughter, and she shares Avery's love for anything princess.) The theme last Christmas was pretty consistent—Cinderella. Cinderella dolls, Cinderella clothes, Cinderella book bags, and more dolls. Disney must be making a fortune . . . from us. You can imagine what I spent a majority of my time doing over the next several months.

It's amazing how long they can sit there and play with those plastic dolls. They must be far more creative than I, because I start to get a little wild after about thirty minutes of making up princess dialogue. One moment has Cinderella complimenting Ariel's beautiful dancing; the next has her giving a head fake and shooting a beautiful double-leg takedown. Ariel always seems caught off guard; Avery always looks at me as if I'm crazy.

I do know that I'm crazy about my daughters. I love spending time with them. If it means being immersed in a world that's completely foreign to me, well, bring it on. Perhaps I'm as awkward as Uncle Si (of the TV show, *Duck Dynasty*) in heels as I play dolls, but they seem to enjoy my company. After I get them laughing really hard, I usually try and steal a hug. The key is to time it out right. They typically respond by pulling away because I'm distracting them from more princess talk. Sometimes Avery will even say, *"Dad, I'm trying to play."* What was I thinking, trying to distract her from her busy play schedule to show my love and affection?

I gave Sophie a bear hug recently—the kind of hug designed to leave no doubt in her little heart that she's deeply loved—and I said, *"Sophie, I wish you knew how much I love you."* In that moment, the Father whispered to my heart: *I know what you mean. I wish you knew how much I love you.* I continued to hug Sophie, and the Father continued to speak: *I wish you would let me love you like that.*

His words penetrated. I realized that God desires to show me affection the way I desire to do so for my daughters. I also realized that I often brush it off because I'm distracted by busyness. I can only imagine the Father smiling and saying: *What was I thinking, trying to distract you from your busy life to show you my love and affection?*

I've since developed a practice of regularly pausing for the express purpose of allowing the Father to love me. I carve out space and clear my mind and heart of everything besides Him. In faith, I picture Him wrapping

His strong arms around me and giving me a bear hug. My heart smiles every time. I think He smiles every time.

Knowing about the Father's love is not enough; you need to experience it. You were created to be loved in a deeply personal way by a deeply personal Father. Your heart must experience this, or it will slowly grow hard. If you're heart is already hard, then you need it all the more. Far too many people never allow the idea of God's love to move beyond the cognitive level. They've spent their lives singing "Jesus Loves Me," but their hearts keep a safe distance from the all-consuming truth. I suspect the primary reason is they simply don't believe they deserve it.

This is a lie that must be dealt with.

A LIFE-CHANGING EXPERIENCE

I grew up around the sport of wrestling. Some of my earliest memories are from spending Saturday mornings in a gymnasium, watching my "heroes" wrestle. Many people who hear "wrestling" and "heroes" probably think of Hulk Hogan, Sting, Andre the Giant, and the rest of the crazed men who once sported a Speedo and face paint. I'm actually talking about names like Degood, VanDyke, Lampe, and the other young men I watched endure the excruciating work needed to become great high school wrestlers. I was young, but I took notice.

As I watched those guys wrestle, I began dreaming of the day I would compete and wrestle in front of a packed Gross Memorial Coliseum at the state tournament. My ten-year-old squirrely body would often—in the privacy of my own bedroom—rehearse my response to hearing the final buzzer sound in my imaginary state championship match. I would get up, throw my arms in the air, and thank God for the victory. I had no idea if I would actually ever experience this in real life, but it was a dream.

The small spark that was initially lit from watching great high school wrestlers compete when I was a young boy was fanned into flame by my dad. He spent countless hours helping young men become great wrestlers—over thirty years coaching the sport. He saw my dream, and he was equally committed to helping me attain it.

When I was in sixth grade, I attended a wrestling camp at the University of Iowa. In addition to driving me to the camp—it must have seemed like eternal distances, driving across the Great Plains of the Midwest—my parents shelled out hundreds of dollars to pay for the camp. I walked around the campus amazed at the men I was encountering. *Wow*, I thought to myself, *there is Dan Gable!* I was starstruck. Similar to a teenage girl at a Taylor Swift concert, I was in awe of seeing the people whose pictures appeared on posters that hung all over my bedroom wall. In the midst of collecting autographs, I also managed to learn a few new moves. Most importantly, I jotted something down in a little notebook that would serve to motivate me for the next ten years. In messy sixth grade handwriting, I had written, "My goal is to be an All-American."

I had a lot of dreams as a kid. Many of them were a little "out there." I proudly announced at my sixth grade graduation that my life goal was to become the middle linebacker for the Denver Broncos. Although I eventually swallowed the bitter pill and acknowledged the fact that my 150-pound frame wasn't suited for the NFL, I couldn't let go of my dream to be an All-American wrestler.

Being an All-American is attained by placing in the top eight at a national tournament. My mom and dad were faithful to drive me all over the country during my high school years to give me the opportunity to accomplish my goal. It was also common for them to drive seventeen hours only to watch me lose two matches and then spend another seventeen hours driving me home.

I had success in high school at the state level and eventually became a state champion. As sweet as the victory was, I couldn't forget about my childhood goal of placing at a national tournament. I took the plunge and decided to wrestle in college. It didn't take long for me to realize that college wrestling is a different animal.

Halfway into my freshman year, I called my dad to announce I was quitting the team. His response was something that I can still hear ringing in my ears. "Son," he said, "you need to finish what you started." Being in college put me in a position where I didn't technically have to listen to my dad's advice. However, he had earned my respect as a man and as a coach. I chose to listen to his advice, and I continued to grind along. I managed to barely qualify for the national tournament, and sure enough, my parents endured the marathon drive to Minnesota to support me. The result was the same as previous years. I found myself beat up, discouraged, and quickly out of the tournament after losing two matches.

It wasn't looking good for me to attain my goal, but I decided to wrestle for one more year. I had mediocre success during the regular season and just barely qualified for the national tournament for the second straight year. I wasn't ranked. I was largely unnoticed and certainly not expected to do much at the national tournament. To be honest, as bad as I wanted it, I really didn't expect it to happen either.

I always got nervous when I heard my name announced, indicating that it was time to head to my mat assignment. *Let the final tournament of my seventeen year career begin,* I thought to myself as I heard my name come across the booming loud speakers. When I arrived at my assigned mat, I looked over and evaluated my competition. He appeared to be bigger, stronger, and more confident than me. He was nationally ranked and expected to be an All-American. Most people who knew the sport expected him to cruise through his first match (yes, against me).

Lacking confidence, I looked across the coliseum and spotted my dad who had worked his way into a front row seat. Seeing him gave me confidence. The look on his face communicated that he really expected me to win. What was wrong with him?! Had he already forgotten about all of the other years? Did he really expect that this year would be different?

I walked on the mat, shook my opponent's hand, and within the first minute, found myself flying through the air only to experience an abrupt thump as my head bounced off the mat. Worse than the pain was the reality that I was on the verge of being pinned—and humiliated. I halfheartedly fought off my back and considered giving up. My mind instantly started replaying the same old thoughts: *Here you go again. It's not going to happen.*

Give up and get this over with.

Somehow, I managed to fight off my back and even scored a reversal as we went off the mat. As I walked back to the center, I heard something that will forever be with me. It was the sound of my dad's voice as he yelled, "Come on, son. Fight!" I can't explain it, but something inside me came alive. Confidence flooded my soul.

I was taken aback by his boldness. I think the entire section of the coliseum heard him. How embarrassing it would have been for him to boldly support me only to watch me come up short again. Usually fans of an inevitable loser sink down into their chairs and pretend to not know the sorry competitor. My dad was the opposite. He stood up and offered his support when I needed it the most. He believed in me, and it did something in me. The words that carried across the floor of the coliseum and overpowered the voices of hundreds of other fans ignited something in me that needed to be lit.

The faded dream of becoming an All-American suddenly became clear again. With a renewed sense of direction and passion, I fought back to pull out an upset win, 8-7. This was a defining moment in my life. My eyes were opened to see that the story doesn't always have to follow the same shipwrecked script.

I won my next match 10-8, which put me one win away from becoming an All-American. I can't explain the feeling I experienced when it dawned on me that this might actually happen. I got away by myself and prepared for the most important match of my career.

I was nervous but optimistic as I stepped on the mat.

I didn't have a chance to see where my mom and dad were seated, but I was sure I would soon hear my dad—and so would the rest of the fans in the arena.

The first two periods were close and hard fought, but I trailed the entire time. I was a man on a mission in the third and final period, but my opponent defended well. He simply had to hold on for ten more seconds in order to seal the victory and crush my dreams. In what felt like a miraculous moment, I snapped him to the mat and shucked him by to score a last second winning take down.

The moments after hearing the final buzzer sound were surreal. Time seemed to slow down. My coach started jumping all over the place, and I simply lifted my arms in the air—a lot like what I had rehearsed as a ten-year-old. I looked over to see my dad running towards me with open arms. He ran right past the security guard—who was supposed to ensure that parents remained in the stands—but there was nothing stopping my dad. He picked me up and gave me the greatest bear hug of my life. Tears were flowing from each of our eyes as we embraced the moment that had eluded us for years. He kissed me on the cheek and then picked me up again for another bear hug.

It has been several years since that experience, and I still think about it often. As much as I wanted to become an All-American, that's not what I remember about that day. I remember the joy I felt from making my dad proud. He was delighted, and because of it, so was I.

My post victory bear hug from my dad was far more than a simple demonstration of joy. It felt divine. I would later realize that God wanted to use this exact moment to teach me a powerful truth. God spoke to my heart: *That's how I treat you every day. There's not a day that goes by that I don't desire to show you that kind of love and affection. I want to embrace you after your greatest victory and your worst defeat. I'm quite proud of you, and you simply can't do anything to change that.*

This has been a radical shift in how I approach God as a Father. For years, I assumed God was only delighted in me if I acted a certain way. I knew better than to say it out loud, but deep within me, I believed I had to earn God's affection. This assumption wasn't congruent with what God was teaching me, and it certainly didn't line up with the truth of Scripture.

THE PRODIGAL SON'S EXPERIENCE

The prodigal son is a man who experienced the greatest bear hug of his life after his worst defeat. In Luke 15, we see Jesus teaching His disciples about the true heart of His Father. The rebellious young man in the story asked for his inheritance early—essentially issuing a death wish for his father—and set his sights on a distant land where he proceeded to waste everything on wild living.

And not many days later, the younger son gathered everything together and went on a journey into a distant country, and there he squandered his estate with loose living. Now when he had spent everything, a severe famine occurred in that country, and he began to be impoverished. So he

went and hired himself out to one of the citizens of that country, and he sent him into his fields to feed swine. And he would have gladly filled his stomach with the pods that the swine were eating, and no one was giving anything to him. But when he came to his senses, he said, "How many of my father's hired men have more than enough bread, but I am dying here with hunger! I will get up and go to my father, and will say to him, 'Father, I have sinned against heaven, and in your sight; I am no longer worthy to be called your son; make me as one of your hired men.'"
(Luke 15:13-19, NASB)

The son probably rehearsed his speech all the way home. How would his father receive him? Would his father return the death wish upon his son? Would the son be permanently banished from the family? Would he be scourged and whipped? Tar and feathered? Hung upside down by his toenails? He didn't know what kind of welcome he would receive, but he decided to go anyway.

So he got up and came to his father. But while he was still a long way off, his father saw him and felt compassion for him, and ran and embraced him and kissed him. (Luke 15:20, NASB)

This is one of the most striking moments in Scripture. Can you picture it? The father looking off in the distance, hoping and praying to one day see his son return. Day after day, he retires to bed without seeing his dream morph into reality. Perhaps he returns to the window one final time each night just to make sure he's not missing the answer to countless prayers.

The father knew that if he didn't watch intently, his son would experience the Kezazeh ceremony. This was a custom during first century Jewish culture of which Jesus' original audience would have been well aware. Kenneth Bailey has spent forty years studying Middle Eastern culture, and he provides insight into the Kezazah ceremony, writing:

> First century Jewish custom dictated that if a Jewish boy lost the family inheritance among the Gentiles and dared to return home, the community would break a large pot in front of him and cry out "so-in-so is cut off from his people." This ceremony was called the *Kezazah (literally "the cutting off")*. After it was performed, the community would have nothing to do with the wayward person.[1]

The fact that the father *ran* towards the son is amazing. In that culture, during that time, it was unheard of for a distinguished man over the age of twenty-five to run anywhere. It was considered a shameful and humiliating act. Property owners only walked in a slow, dignified manner.

The father hiked up his robe, exposed his legs, and ran for his son. He took the humiliation the son deserved and placed it upon himself—something we also see at the cross. I'm sure there were many people who tried to stop him along the way. After all, the villagers wanted to see the Kezazah ceremony, they wanted justice. There was no stopping the father though.

The father embraced the son. The Greek word for *embraced* is "epipipto." This means, "to fall upon; to seize possession of." (Greek is the original language of the New Testament.) The father was seizing possession of the son before he could be cut off by the community. Through the cross, God was seizing possession of us before we would be cut off for eternity. The father's bear hug was designed to leave little doubt in the son's heart that he was deeply loved, that he belonged to the father. Our Heavenly Father wants to remove all doubt from our hearts as well.

The best picture I have for this is the way my dad embraced me after my All-American match. Tears in his eyes, beaming with an indescribable joy, and ready to celebrate! He didn't kill the fattened calf, but he did take me to Red Lobster. I sat across the table and enjoyed the delight of my father. The prodigal son surely experienced a similar delight as the father threw him the party of all parties. The best meat was prepared, a robe and ring were given, and dancing and music erupted from the house. The only thing louder than the music was the statement being declared: Sonship surpasses behavior.

Our position as a son or daughter isn't changed because of our sin. In fact, being a son or daughter actually positions us to experience freedom from sin and bondage. However, we have to understand the true nature of the Father.

After we sin, isn't it common to mope around and think the Father is upset at us? *I really blew it again,* we think to ourselves as we feel the sting of guilt and regret. Perhaps we assume the Father is sinking down in His chair, embarrassed to affiliate Himself with such sorry losers. And it's in this moment that the enemy prompts us to run farther and farther from God. We separate ourselves from the only one who can truly help us.

I'm reminded of a bird that recently flew into our garage and got stuck. I spent twenty minutes trying to free the bird, trying to help it return to a glorious life of flying and freedom. I didn't have any harmful intentions, but the bird didn't trust me. It spent the next several minutes trying desperately to escape my help, but only ended up smacking itself into walls, paint cans, and rakes. I finally helped the bird achieve freedom, but the pain and suffering would have been much less if it would have allowed me to help from the beginning. The experience helped me see from the Father's perspective. How often do we get caught in bondage, and then flee from the one trying to help? Instead of allowing shame and guilt to drive us away from the Father, let's allow repentance to draw us near.

The Father doesn't have any harmful intentions towards you—even after you sin. He just wants to help you achieve a glorious life of freedom.

This is what He sees when He looks at you. He sees the potential for deep freedom. He sees a son or daughter that He delights in. You are the object of His affection and the apple of His eye. He doesn't view you the way you view yourself, nor does He treat you the way you treat yourself.

Blaise Pascal wrote, "God made man in His own image and man returned the compliment." Brennan Manning adds, "And so we unwittingly project onto God our own attitudes and feelings toward ourselves." This often happens at a deep subconscious level, but it's a cruel act against the Father. We're essentially saying, *I don't believe you could be so good, so I'm going to tell you who you really are.*

Who am I to tell God who He is? I've been guilty of this grievous error, and I know I'm not alone. So much of the dysfunctional behavior I've tried to help people correct in counseling can be traced back to a dysfunctional view of God and self. We develop an image of a God that makes sense, but it's a false god. As long as we wallow in our shame, assuming the Father wants nothing to do with us, or assuming He has harmful intentions towards us, we bow to a false god. The longer we bow to these false gods by abiding in our negative beliefs, the more we'll forfeit His true goodness.

Remember, it's God's goodness that changes us. His kindness leads us to repentance (Romans 2:4). The design is for His nature to change our nature, not the other way around. So allow Him to love you right where you are. He stands willing and ready today to reveal His affection for you. His arms are open. He invites you to draw near and embrace the bear hug.

7.
HOUND OF HEAVEN

As we go deeper into the heart of the Father, we'll find a matchless level of kindness. It's a kindness that often manifests through generosity. The Father delights in being generous to His children. Isn't this what we just witnessed with the prodigal son? The father went above and beyond anything that could have possibly been expected. I wish I could have seen the expression on the faces of those who watched the father pull out the robe and ring. I bet there were a few jaws that hit the floor.

I'm also willing to bet the younger son's heart was turned towards the father. Kindness—especially underserved kindness—has the powerful capacity to affect us at the heart level. Kindness penetrates even the hardest of hearts. God understands this, and He uses His kindness to lead us to repentance (Romans 2:4). Not all hearts are instantly turned towards the Father as a result of His generosity though—especially if the generosity is directed elsewhere.

Now his older son was in the field, and when he came and approached the house, he heard music and dancing. And he summoned one of the servants and began inquiring what these things could be. And he said to him, "Your brother has come, and your father has killed the fattened calf because he has received him back safe and sound." But he became angry and was not willing to go in; and his father came out and began pleading with him. (Luke 15:26-28, NASB)

The elder son, even after all those years, still didn't understand the heart of his father. He assumed that the father's generosity towards his brother meant there would be less for him to enjoy. His jealousy and anger were a result of his narrow perspective. He didn't take a step back and look at the situation through the eyes of his loving father. He proceeded to detail the years of his selfless service, eventually providing an exclamation point with this statement: *And yet you have never given me a young goat, so that I might celebrate with my friends* (Luke 15:29, NASB). The father listened patiently and then responded with an intriguing declaration:

And he said to him, "Son, you have always been with me, and all that is mine is yours."
(Luke 15:31, NASB)

Those six words, "all that is mine is yours," uncover another layer of the Heavenly Father's extravagant generosity. The father stated that he didn't have "mine" and "yours" categories. The older brother was a son, so he was granted access to all that the father possessed.

I've always wondered what happened next? Did the older son show up the next day with a new Ferrari? Did he sport a new designer robe? (Is that missing the point?)

Many people automatically correlate generosity with the giving of material possessions; however, the Heavenly Father's generosity towards us surpasses the bestowment of mere possessions—although He does delight in doing that, too. He has given something far more valuable than money, vehicles, or clothing; He's given His Son, and He's given His Spirit. He's offered Himself.

The true generosity of the Father is seen in the fact that He has given us full access to Himself. He's torn the curtain in two, swung open the palace doors, and invited us to come and enjoy Him—for eternity. This is important to understand if we are to experience deeper levels of His generosity (talk about deep water—you'll never reach the bottom of that ocean). He wants to bless your socks off, but He doesn't want His presents to distract you from His presence. He's ultimately after intimacy with you. His generosity is designed to turn your heart towards Him, resulting in a greater understanding of who He truly is. He's not interested in blessing us to then watch us become obsessed with materialism.

It's also important to understand that part of the reason we're blessed is so we can bless others. Abraham tasted of God's extravagant generosity, but the Bible says he was "blessed to be a blessing" (Genesis 12:2). God's plan was to heap abundant blessings upon Abraham and then watch Abraham reveal the goodness of God to others. The same thing is still happening today.

My phone rang yesterday, and I picked up to hear the sound of my wife in an uproar. She could barely catch her breath. My first thought was that something bad had happened to our kids. Were they safe? Were they behaving? Did Avery and Sophie paint the kitchen wall again? Ashley just kept saying: *"God is so good. God is so good."* After catching her breath from high-stepping around the living room (I rubbed off on her), she explained that someone had sent us a check . It was an extraordinary amount of money, and it was an underserved gift from a friend.

After thanking the Father for His tremendous gift, we asked Him how we could participate. Our hearts were drawn even deeper into His heart of kindness, and we wanted to offer the same opportunity for someone else.

This is a fun way to live. Not only is it refreshing to experience the generosity of the Father, but it aggravates the enemy to no end. Satan despises the kindness of God, primarily because he understands the impact it has on the human heart. He constantly loses ground as people increasingly discover the kindness of the Father.

RECOGNIZING THE KINDNESS

The enemy's strategy is simple: to distract you and blind you from seeing God's kindness. He is quick to remind you of all that is *wrong* with your life so you'll be oblivious to God's generosity. He'll whisper: *"God may be generous to others, but look at your life. Look at your bank account. Real generosity, huh?"* Meanwhile, God is faithfully serving up His kindness and generosity on a daily basis. It may not necessarily be a random check in the mail, or a new car that shows up in your driveway, but do you recognize everything else He's doing? Do you see how He's revealing His generous heart today? We need to pray for eyes that truly see.

David was a man who experienced the generosity of God, but he also had his fair share of hardship. He had an entire army hunting him like a wild dog. Death encircled him on numerous occasions. In one of the most famous chapters of the Bible, David writes:

Even though I walk through the valley of the shadow of death,
I fear no evil, for You are with me;
Your rod and Your staff, they comfort me.
You prepare a table before me in the presence of my enemies;
You have anointed my head with oil;
My cup overflows.
Surely goodness and loving kindness will follow me all the days of my life,
And I will dwell in the house of the LORD forever.
(Psalm 23:4-6, NASB)

David acknowledged the dark valleys; they were quite real to him. He was also quick to recognize the goodness of God in the midst of the troubling physical circumstances. He stated, *You prepare a table before me in the presence of my enemies* (Psalm 23:5, NASB). He didn't just see the army that wanted to rid the earth of him, he saw the God that wanted to shower him with goodness in front of his enemies. He wasn't referencing a sprinkling of kindness when he said, "my cup overflows." Then he declared, *Surely goodness and loving kindness will follow me all the days of my life* (Psalm 23:6, NASB).

David was being pursued by something much more powerful than an army of haters; he was being pursued by the hound of heaven.

This is the same God who pursues you with His goodness and loving kindness. The hound has His eyes on you. Seeing it, though, is a different manner. Recognizing the goodness of God in your life requires intentionality. You have to have your eyes open. Have you seen anything today that reminded you of your generous Father? I'm looking out the window now, and I see an expansive and endless blue sky. It's a simple reminder of His extravagance and generosity.

My daughter, Avery, is teaching me to look for God's goodness, even on ordinary days. She was recently playing in the backyard, when she shouted, *"Thank you, Jesus!"* I turned around and asked her what all the excitement was about. She replied, *"Look at the sunset Jesus created!"* I could see the wonder in her eyes, and I instantly asked God to create the same thing in mine.

Avery has inspired Ashley and I to develop a saying around our home. When we sense the goodness of God—even in seemingly little things—we'll say, *"My cup overflows."* We've discovered that we see a lot more of God's kindness when we're actually looking for it. It's a practice that has deepened our adoration and worship of the Father.

We also talk about the different ways we saw God smile throughout the day. I was driving home recently when I looked over and saw the moon in the perfect shape of a smile. I didn't think anything of it—the sun rays land on the lunar surface, often making the exact same shape—but then I heard the Father speak: *I'm smiling at you. I delight in you.* I responded in worship.

Some may think I'm making something out of nothing, and that the moon's shape had nothing to do with God. I understand where you're coming from. There was a time when I would have thought the same. However, I believe God's kindness towards us can manifest through a variety of ways. He created the natural forces that govern night and day, so why can't He use what He created to communicate to His beloved? If we think He can't do this, our view of Him is way too limited.

I'm not trying to over-spiritualize life by attributing every detail to God. If I push my coffee cup off my desk, I'm not saying God spilled my coffee. There are choices that I make, and there are natural consequences to my choices. The key is growing in our discernment so we can recognize when God is up to something, even if it's through ordinary, everyday events.

Pause and take in your surroundings. What do you see in this moment? Do you see anything that you've never noticed before? Do you see anything that reminds you of God's goodness? Give the Father permission to direct your attention for the rest of the day, and ask Him to highlight His generosity and kindness.

The more you do this, the more you'll see what you didn't previously see. Life will become increasingly rich as you watch your own cup overflow. You may even develop childlike wonder and blurt out your own *"Thank you, Jesus!"*

8.

BITTER KINDNESS

I made a call this week to have the yard aerated. To be honest, I had no idea what benefit aerating the grass had, but I still made the call and wrote the check. I have since done some research and learned that it's incredibly healthy for the soil. In a nutshell, it's the removal of soil plugs in order to increase the water, nutrient, and oxygen movement into the soil. *Something needs to be removed so that something much needed can enter.* The result is a much healthier yard.

A recently aerated lawn is an interesting sight. It looks like a person has neglected to clean up after their dog for the past decade. When I was a young boy, one of my weekly chores included going on "poop patrol." I believe I became quite proficient at searching the yard—while watching my steps very closely—scooping and disposing of the treasure in record time.

Very early on in my scooping career, I remember picking up a shovel and walking to the back yard only to see a sight that no eight-year-old pooper-scooper wants to see. My parents had just had the lawn aerated, but to me, it looked like every dog in a five mile radius had met on our yard and left me a present. I stood there in disbelief. I glanced at the neighbor's yard to see if they were also the recipients of the dog party, but their yard was spotless. How could this be? Was this some sort of bad joke?

Now that I'm older, I look back and smile on that day. My lack of understanding into lawn aeration led me to believe that my eight-year-old life had just become a lot worse. In reality, what I thought was a horrible sight was actually quite healthy for the yard—and good for me. I believe I dismissed myself of my duties that day, claiming I couldn't tell the difference between the dog's mess and the aeration. My initial reaction was clearly misguided.

That wasn't the last time my initial reaction to something has been off. I've made many mistakes and misdiagnosed many circumstances over the years. The more I evaluate these situations, the more I realize that I sometimes labeled the Father's kindness as cruelty.

During my college years, I had a relationship crumble around me. I was deeply invested in the relationship and had thought it would most likely end in marriage. In the depths of my heart, I knew the relationship wasn't what God wanted, but I chose to ignore the truth. The longer I was in the relationship, the less I desired to know God. I was essentially choosing the woman over God, but I also prayed and ask God to sustain the relationship. He was too kind to answer that prayer.

The pain involved with the removal of the relationship was tough. I was devastated. I literally took my phone and threw it across the room as I blamed God for breaking my heart. *"Are you happy now?"* I asked with a smugness that now makes me cringe in embarrassment. The pain blinded me to see it as a deep act of kindness. In that case, *the relationship needed to be removed so that something much needed could enter—God.* The result was a much healthier heart.

I've seen the same basic thing happen in many counseling sessions. As humans, we're often drawn to unhealthy and destructive behaviors. Our sinful nature craves the opposite of what the Spirit desires, creating an internal tug-of-war. If we submit to our sinful nature, we'll form unhealthy and sometimes dangerous attachments. In my case, I had formed an unhealthy attachment to an unhealthy relationship. It's also true that we have a Father who wants to remove them, not because He enjoys watching us suffer, but because He wants to create room for immense blessing.

I was reminded of this truth a few weeks ago. I took Avery on a daddy-daughter date, and I sat across the table from her and was taken aback by how her blue eyes were shining so brightly in the light. As we talked, laughed, and made a mess, I noticed a song that happened to be playing on the radio in the background. It was a song that reminded me of my former relationship. It was quite evident to me that the pain was long gone, and instead of anger at God, I couldn't stop praising Him. God knew what He was doing after all. All I had to do is look across the table and into the eyes of my daughter to be reminded of His faithfulness. I drove home and embraced my wife with a hug and kiss, and thanked God for His amazing kindness to me.

CAN DISCIPLINE BE AN ACT OF KINDNESS?

God's kindness doesn't always appear kind. Any parent knows there are times that you have to say NO to your children. *"No, you can't eat the entire plate of sugar cookies." "No, you can't play video games until your eyeballs fall out." "No, you can't stay out until 3 a.m."* There are other times when parents have to ask children to do things they may not want to do: *"Yes, you need to eat your vegetables." "Yes, you need to go to school today." "Yes, you need to scoop poop in the back yard."* The reality is that parents see a bigger picture than children, so we have to use our authority to guide them down the right path—even when they think we're just being a killjoy.

An important part of the guiding process involves discipline. A parent disciplines a child out of love. The Bible explains, *Whoever spares the rod hates their children, but the one who loves their children is careful to discipline them* (Proverbs 13:24, NIV). Discipline is ultimately an act of kindness. (I'm referencing godly discipline, not abuse or neglect.) However, it's rarely received as an act of kindness from the child.

I remember hearing my dad say, "Gabe, I love you, but I'm going to have to give you a swat because of your poor choices." Those are the words no young boy wants to hear. At the same time, I deserved every paddling I ever received. I can now recognize the Scriptures were talking about me by declaring: *Foolishness is bound up in the heart of a child; The rod of discipline will remove it far from him"* (Proverbs 22:15, NASB).

I didn't concede at the time that I deserved the spanking. In fact, before I received the discipline, I always backed away to perform a speech worthy of an Academy Award.

"Dad," I would start with a look of sincerity in my eyes, "before you give me a spanking, I want you to know that you are the best dad in the world." I would glance at the floor and then back at him, praying my words were penetrating and landing in his heart: "I am just so thankful to have you as a dad!"

As moving as my speech must have been, he always seemed unmoved by my Oscar worthy performance. In a calm and steady manner, he would always respond, "Gabe, I love you, too," (causing my eyes to brighten as I wondered if I was going to get out of it), "which is why I am going to give you a spanking" (plan failed).

The next scene had me receiving a spanking, jumping around the living room, yelping like an injured hyena and running to my room in protest. In the moment, I certainly didn't view the spanking as an act of kindness.

Now, I have a deep respect for my father, and I'm very thankful he possessed the courage and consistency to discipline me. I shudder at the thought of where I would be today if not for the faithful discipline I received as a young boy.

It's been a long time since I've been disciplined by my earthly father, but God still disciplines me from time to time. It's odd, but I find comfort in His discipline. For it's in His rebuke that I see how much He cares. It's one way He reminds us that we are His true children.

It is for discipline that you endure; God deals with you as with sons; for what son is there whom his father does not discipline? But if you are without discipline, of which all have become partakers, then you are illegitimate children and not sons. Furthermore, we had earthly fathers to discipline us, and we respected them; shall we not much rather be subject to the Father of spirits, and live? For they disciplined us for a short time as seemed best to them, but He disciplines us for our good, so that we may share His holiness. All discipline for the moment seems not to be joyful, but sorrowful; yet to those who have been trained by it, afterwards it yields the peaceful fruit of righteousness.
(Hebrews 12:7-11, NASB)

Not only is discipline designed to create healthy and appropriate boundaries for your own protection and well-being, but it "yields the peaceful fruit of righteousness." The Father uses discipline to form you into His image. He is busy pruning away the unfruitful branches to make room for increased fruit (John 15). Sometimes, it's a painful process.

It's easy to resist this process because of the pain and discomfort involved; however, if we continually resist and buck like a wild stallion, we'll end up in a much worse place. Untamable horses usually end up in the slaughter house, but horses that learn to submit to the master enjoy a pretty nice life. Solomon addressed unsubmitted people by stating:

Therefore, they must eat the bitter fruit of living their own way, choking on their own schemes.
(Proverbs 1:31, NLT)

Discipline may initially taste bitter, but it's nothing compared to the bitter fruit that remains in the life of someone who refuses to be corrected. In fact, Scripture explains *a person will die for lack of instruction, And in the greatness of his folly he will go astray* (Proverbs 5:23, NASB). The Father loves you too much to remain silent while you march right off an unseen cliff. This is why He is so committed to the process of discipline and correction, even if you label it as cruelty.

LEARNING FROM JESUS' EXAMPLE

So how can we learn to cooperate with the process? How can we stay submitted to the Father's will, even if it is a bitter cup to drink?

Jesus modeled this in a perfect manner. In Mark 14, we see Him struggling in prayer moments before the arresting band of civilized barbarians arrive and take Him away. Jesus looked at His disciples and said, *My soul is deeply grieved to the point of death; remain here and keep watch* (Mark 14:34, NASB). Jesus was well aware of the bitter cup that had been prepared for Him, and it was taking quite a toll on Him.

Because of His humanity, Jesus could have retreated from the Father and doubted His goodness. He could have said, *I've served you my entire life, and this is how you treat me . . . some Father you are!* The years of intimacy between the Father and Son could have been swept away in those moments of distress.

Jesus didn't retreat from the Father; He moved towards the Father. He called out, *"Abba, Father!"* The word, "Abba," means "Papa" or "Daddy." It's a phrase loaded with intimacy. Jesus maintained intimacy with the Father in the midst of His darkest hour. His relationship with the Father wasn't dependent upon the unfolding of life's troubling events.

At the same time, it was the intimacy that Jesus shared with the Father that allowed Him to freely ask that the cup be removed. He didn't entertain that thought long though, because the next moment has Him saying, "yet not what I will, but what you will" (Mark 14:36).

The Scripture only allows us to see from Jesus' perspective, but can you imagine what the Father was feeling? His Son was calling out, *"Daddy!"* It was the love and kindness for humanity that restrained the Father from acting. The cup was unimaginably bitter for each of them, but it was the greatest act of kindness the world has ever seen.

God knows what it's like to endure the bitter cup. He's a God who knows exactly what it's like to walk in our shoes and experience pain and suffering. This is why it's important to draw closer to Him during challenging and trying times rather than away.

It's easy to punch my keys and type these things, but I'm fully aware that it's much harder to live this truth in the heat of the moment. I sat with a good friend recently and listened to him describe the previous seven months of his life. They've been hellacious.

It started with a broken finger suffered while serving at his church. On his way home that night, he slid on black ice and wrecked his truck. His wife hit her head in the accident and suffered neurological damage. A few days later, their daughter became extremely sick and had to be rushed to the hospital. The doctors discovered that her appendix had ruptured and they immediately took her in for a dangerous surgery.

I remembered sitting with him in the waiting room, tears filling his eyes as he waited patiently for the results of the surgery. It was only supposed to take ninety minutes, but we were still waiting after three hours. In the meantime, the only news he had heard was unsettling— the doctors said it was much worse than they initially thought. Nobody really knew if she would make it or not.

The doctor eventually walked around the corner and delivered the news that she had survived. He said, "It looked like a bomb went off in her, but she's going to make it." My friend experienced a surge of relief and joy, and after several more days in the hospital, they were headed home—exhausted.

Little did they know, the fire they had been walking through was about to become even more real. The home they returned to was in the direct path of the Black Forest fire—which became the most destructive wildfire in Colorado history. The evacuation call came and they were forced to grab a few belongings and leave their house. The waiting game was brutal. They checked the Internet frequently for reports. Their hope began to diminish as they received news that the fire department had abandoned their post in their neighborhood because the flames were too hot. They received news that homes were lost on their street, but didn't know if their home was still standing or among the over 500 homes lost.

The fire literally followed their property line, but left their house untouched. Though my friend was saddened for his neighbors, he was relieved that his house was spared. While the fire didn't scorch his property, the fire of life was still seemingly roaring out of control, threatening to reduce him to a pile of blackened embers.

Shortly after the fire, the government shutdown occurred. He had recently purchased a company that was very dependent upon government contracts. The shutdown placed its ugly hands around the throat of his company and threatened his financial security. Uncertainty swirled around him at every turn.

Meanwhile, his father-in-law suffered a major heart attack. This man he loved deeply was left hanging on for dear life. It was yet another blow for a man who was already reeling. His father-in-law slowly recovered, but more medical issues were around the corner for this precious family.

Soon after, his wife was riding a horse when it fell, throwing her to the ground violently. She was injured and in an extraordinary amount of pain. The MRI at the hospital revealed that she had a dislocated pelvis, but the doctors saw something else that was troubling. Apparently, she also had a tumor on her spine that needed to be removed as soon as possible.

I looked across the table and saw something interesting in my friend's eyes as we recounted these trials. It was obvious that he was tired and the previous seven months had taken a toll, but I also saw hope. I saw the eyes of a man who refused to retreat from the Father. He said, "Gabe, I remember the exact moment when I prayed a dangerous prayer. I asked God to form me into His image."

The power of that statement hung in the air. He continued, "This is not easy, but I know God is answering my prayer." He wasn't saying God caused everything (we live in a broken world, and have an enemy), but He was mature enough to realize that God was at work bringing good out of the circumstances, even if he couldn't necessarily see it all.

My friend's statement reminded me of something George Macdonald wrote:

> To give us the spiritual gift we desire, God may have to begin far back in our spirit, in regions unknown to us, and do much work that we can be aware of only in the results . . . In the gulf of our unknown being God works behind our consciousness with His holy influence, with His own presence . . . . He may be approaching our consciousness from behind, coming forward through regions of our darkness into our light, long before we begin to be aware that He is answering our request—has answered it, and is visiting His child.[1]

My friend was aware of certain aspects of God's working—everyone had survived, the house was still standing, and so on—but he knew there was a deeper work taking place, a work occurring in the deep water of his heart. With a look of authenticity, he said, "I'm more aware of the hidden pride in my life than I've ever been." Not only did he refuse to pull back from the Father during the trials, he was actually opening up more of his heart to the Father. It was clear that he harbored a deep trust in God. He was following the model Jesus established—draw near, guard the intimacy, be committed to prayer, and stay submitted to the Father.

Later that night, I invited the Father to search my heart the way my friend was allowing God to search his. *Is there anything in my heart that you want to remove, Father? How are you pruning me? How are you correcting me and forming me into your image?* His answer was quick and concise: *Pride.* It wasn't that I thought I was the greatest thing since sliced bread, but my pride was hidden in self-reliance. The Father wanted to remove this to make room for immense blessing.

I submitted to the Father through repentance, and I asked Him how I could cooperate with the process. His answer was again quick and concise: *Worship.* He was right; the path to deep humility is the path of deep worship. Then I asked Him what blessing He was creating room for, and He said: *Joy.*

One of the best ways for you to experience the kindness of the Father is to allow Him to search your heart and remove what needs to be removed. He'll prune the branches and pull the weeds, creating space for healthy seed.

I encourage you to ask Him the same question: *Father, is there anything in my heart that needs to be removed?*

Give Him plenty of space to answer. If you don't hear anything immediately, stay with the question in the days ahead. He'll surely answer. He loves you too much to remain silent.

He's simply too kind.

SECTION III
THE DEEP WATER
OF YOUR HEART

... the heart of man is like deep water.
(Proverbs 20:5, NKJV)

9.
WHO ARE YOU?

There is a depth to your life beyond your wildest expectations. You are a person of deep substance. You were created in the image of God (Genesis 1:27), and His heart is deep water. What does that say about you? Weren't you crafted in His likeness? We can conclude that bearing His image accurately requires us to live from the depth of our redeemed hearts, the place He fashioned to represent His being.

It's also true that many of us are living a shadow of the life we were created for, because we don't know what lies in the deep water of our hearts. It's unchartered territory; it's the "gulf of the unknown." We're not quite sure who we truly are. We may have a foggy idea—some more than others—but there is always room to discover more and more of the glory God has placed upon and within our lives.

We live in a culture in which it's easy to want to emulate others. How often do we compare ourselves to others and find ourselves wishing we were more like them?

The longer we harbor these thoughts the more likely it is we'll start to force ourselves to act like them (even if it's subtle and subconscious); all the while neglecting the glory that God has placed upon our unique lives. I once heard a man say, "If you truly knew who you were created to be, you would never want to be someone else."

I can't help but think God has given you a unique deposit designed to glorify Him in a way that nobody else can. The more we understand how unique we are as individuals, the more we'll be in awe of the Creator. Allowing God to search and reveal our hearts isn't designed to lead to self-worship; its purpose is to lead to real worship of the one who created us. What painter creates a masterpiece and then proceeds to hide it? The Scripture says you are God's "masterpiece" (Ephesians 2:10). You are the one who has been "fearfully and wonderfully" made (Psalm 139). His desire is to uncover and display this masterpiece.

The Greek word used in the New Testament for "heart" is "kardia," meaning: "the center of all physical and spiritual life." It references the center or core of who we are. It's a term used over 150 times in the New Testament, including the following verse:

> He who searches the hearts knows what the mind of the Spirit is, because He intercedes for the saints according to the will of God. (Romans 8:27, NASB)

Like a deep sea submersion vehicle, God searches the deep water of your heart. There's nothing hidden from His sight. The thought of God knowing the deepest, darkest secrets of your heart may be unnerving, but it's actually really good news. When the light of Jesus shines in your heart, darkness is forced to flee. This is why my prayer is: *God, shine your light in the deepest regions of my heart.*

This is an intriguing and powerful prayer. God will proceed to shine His light in your heart, and the result will be that you gain a deeper understanding of who you were always meant to be. God will reveal what's ultimately true about your heart, and He'll work to align your life so it reflects this truth.

The process of learning to live from our hearts requires courage and authenticity. We have to be willing to take a candid look at ourselves. We may discover that our lives are a lousy representation of what God has placed in our hearts. If this is the case, are we willing to allow Him to rid us of the contradiction?

I believe the process starts with asking a few simple questions: *Who am I? What is true about my God-formed heart?* These are questions geared to reveal your identity.

The Father delights in revealing true identity. After Jesus was baptized, the Father spoke and said, *You are my dearly loved Son, and you bring me great joy* (Luke 3:22, NLT). The Father was talking directly to Jesus—He said "You." If the Father was exclusively speaking for the benefit of the people around Jesus (similar to Mark 8), then He would have said, "This is my Son." If Jesus needed to hear the Father speak identity over Him, how much more do you and I?

One reason this is so important is because the enemy has plenty to say in regard to your identity. He works to challenge and distort your identity at every turn.

He realizes that if he can deceive you on this topic, he can take much ground in your life and conceal the glory of God.

He even challenged Jesus' identity. After His baptism, the Spirit led Jesus into the desert where He was tempted by the evil deceiver. *"If* you are the Son of God," Satan snarled, "Tell this stone to become bread." Jesus wasn't about to fall for the wiles of the enemy, but Satan continued to try anyway. *"If* you are the Son of God, throw yourself down from here." Satan tried to tempt Jesus into proving His identity. It was a direct attack against the Father's words. It didn't work.

It works too often against us, though. Satan is lying to us about who we are. Jesus called Satan the *father of all lies*, and He said, "there is no truth in him" (John 8:44). Have you ever stopped to consider what Satan is saying to you about you? What's he trying to get you to believe about yourself? You may think his accusations are your own thoughts, but you must know that the enemy wants to be deeply involved in the formation of your identity. He'll even use the words of others to solidify what he's saying.

Words spoken by others have a powerful impact on the development of our identity. Many of the people I've had the privilege of counseling have possessed a distorted view of themselves as a direct result of words spoken to them by others. A dear woman in her sixties admitted that she has always felt ugly. It was a phrase she often heard from her peers as a child. The lie remained planted in her heart for nearly four decades, until she heard the Father speak truth.

Her face brightened as she said, "I had no idea that my Heavenly Father loved me this much. I mean," she paused as if to collect her thoughts, "He really likes me. I'm finally realizing what it means to be His daughter!" Her identity was shifting from the ugly and unwanted person to a cherished daughter of God as a result of listening to the Father. Truth's floodgates were opening over her heart, washing the lies away.

Because we were designed by the Father, He's the only one who can truly tell us who we are. When it comes to discovering our identity, He should be granted our undivided attention. He's the only one who really knows what He's placed in the depth of our hearts. Our spouses, parents, children, and good friends may see part of the picture—or in some instances, actually reinforce the lie of the enemy—but only God sees the complete truth, and He's committed to drawing out of you what He's placed in you.

There's a question I often ask in counseling that usually has an impact on people at a deep level. It can be a game changer if you stay with the question until you hear answers. It's a simple question: *How does the Father view you?* Again, I'm trying to help people see through the Father's eyes. I want their identity to be shaped by what the Father sees, not what they see when they look in the mirror. Sometimes people will try and answer the question immediately, and then pause and say, "I'm not really sure." I encourage them to take the question directly to the Father. Sometimes the answer is so surprising that they actually struggle to say it out loud. They're embarrassed because they're so used to believing the opposite.

Understanding your identity—discovering what's true about your heart—is about listening to the words of your Creator. How does He view you? Who does He say you are? Create some space in order to listen. Take the question directly to your loving Father.

CREATED TO SHINE

If you're having a hard time hearing the Father, it doesn't mean something is wrong with you. You must know that there is a fierce battle raging between the kingdom of God and the kingdom of darkness on the topic of your identity. There is much at stake.

We were designed to reflect the glory of God to a world steeped in darkness. God's plan is for us to "arise and shine." The prophet Isaiah captured this truth and painted a beautiful picture with his words:

Arise, shine; for your light has come,
And the glory of the LORD has risen upon you.
 For behold, darkness will cover the earth
And deep darkness the peoples;
But the LORD will rise upon you
And His glory will appear upon you.
Nations will come to your light,
And kings to the brightness of your rising.
(Isaiah 60:1-3, NASB)

Not only does the glory of the Lord shine upon us, but it shines through us. Jesus said, *You are the light of the world. A town built on a hill cannot be hidden. Neither do people light a lamp and put it under a bowl. Instead they put it on its stand, and it gives light to ev-*

eryone in the house. In the same way, let your light shine before others, that they may see your good deeds and glorify your Father in heaven (Matthew 5:14-16, NIV).

There is a direct connection between the light of Jesus shining through our hearts and the Father receiving glory in this dark world. This is why the battle rages on in the spiritual realm. God's primary plan for revealing His glory on planet Earth is through us—Christ in us, the hope of glory (Colossians 1:27). That's a weighty and significant truth. He is urging us to *arise and shine*, to be who we were created to be. The enemy is tempting us to hide and take cover, to not allow anyone to see the truth of who we really are. God is commanding us to step into our God-given destiny and take the territory He's given us. The enemy is prompting us to run away and carve out a much *safer* existence.

A LIFE OF HIDING

This back and forth battle is actually portrayed in *The Lion King*. I'm becoming very familiar with this movie, as it happens to be Avery's new favorite. She sits perfectly still for the entire two hours, hanging on every word. Then she'll spend the rest of the day singing, "Can you feel the love tonight?" I try and redirect her by belting out, "In the jungle, the mighty jungle," but she always gives me "the look." It's a look I'm quite familiar with: *Dad, you really can't sing.*

I must admit, I do enjoy the film. In fact, I had forgotten how much it parallels life. The evil uncle, Scar, uses deception to orchestrate the events leading to King Mufasa's death. Then Scar turns around and blames his work on the young, impressionable cub, Simba. "Run away and never come back," growls Scar the accuser.

In essence, Scar was shaming an innocent Simba. The result was that Simba retreated from his role as son and future king, and he fled to a faraway land. He took to a life of hiding, refusing his destiny and true purpose. Each day Simba spent in hiding was a day the rest of the creatures who called Pride Rock their home suffered.

Enter Rafiki.

Rafiki was a wise old baboon who decided it was only fitting to challenge Simba and remind him of his true identity.

Rafiki: (singing) "Asanta Sane. Squash Banana. We We Nugu. Mi Mi Apana."

Simba: "Enough Already! What's that supposed to mean anyway?"

Rafiki: "It means you're a baboon; and I'm not" (laughter).

Simba: "I think you're a little confused."

Rafiki: "Wrong! I'm not the one who's confused. You don't even know who you are."

Simba: "And I suppose you know?"

Rafiki: "Sure do. You're Mufasa's boy. Bye."[1]

We all need a wise old baboon like Rafiki; a person who refuses to remain silent as we live a shadow of the life we were created to live. In a sense, my dad offered me this reminder during my wrestling match at nationals. He was naming what was true about me. He was calling me back to the truth. The result was that I stepped forward in courage and engaged the battle rather than retreating in fear and timidity.

The same happened with Simba. Rafiki simply helped position Simba in a place where he could hear his father speak, and the result was an awakening. Simba, with a renewed sense of identity, returned to Pride Rock and took back the territory he had given up.

The story of *The Lion King* is essentially a story of the spiritual battle we face. We are sons and daughters of the King. We also have an enemy, an accuser, who actively works against us. He "kills, steals, and destroys," and then he wants to blame his work on us. The result of believing his lies affords the opportunity for shame to enter, and then we retreat and take up a life of hiding. I've seen the same cycle over and over again in counseling. I've even experienced it firsthand in my own life.

I was about five years old when the accusation came. I experienced a traumatic event and the attached message was clear: *You are different. There is something wrong with you. Run away and hide.* Satan was trying to convince me that his work was my fault, that something was wrong with me at my core. Shame entered my soul that day, and my true identity as being fearfully and wonderfully made was replaced by a commitment to prove myself acceptable to others. Because I carried a subtle lie deep in my heart that there was something wrong with me, I constructed an identity built on the wrong foundation. The false Gabe was created.

I didn't recognize it at the time, but I spent a majority of my younger years trying to fit in. One of my biggest fears was rejection, so I proceeded to become the ringleader, the one with the power to decide who would be accepted and who would be rejected. I wasn't living from the redeemed heart of Christ, I was engaging in self-protective behavior.

The fear of rejection continued as I got older, and I adapted by embracing other self-protecting behaviors. I wasn't the mean jerk on the playground; instead I had become a people pleaser, afraid of disappointing others. I wasn't living from the redeemed heart of Christ within me; I was living behind a mask. Ultimately, the reason for the mask was that I still believed the message from my childhood: *Don't show people who you really are. There's something wrong with you. You'll be rejected.*

Brennan Manning wrote:

> When I was eight, the imposter, or false self, was born as a defense against pain. The imposter within whispered, "Brennan, don't ever be your real self anymore because nobody likes you as you are. Invent a new self that everybody will admire and nobody will know." So I became a good boy— polite, well-mannered, unobtrusive, and deferential. I studied hard, scored excellent grades, won a scholarship in high school, and was stalked every waking moment by the terror of abandonment and the sense that nobody was there for me.[2]

The tragedy is that the true heart is essentially forced to go into hiding as the false self is given more freedom to dominate. The projected image we present to others is only solidified as it's rewarded by the acceptance and praise of others. This acceptance feels good, so we learn to crave it at a deep level. In *Way of the Heart*, Henri Nouwen writes:

Why do we children of the light so easily become conspirators with the darkness? The answer is quite simple. Our identity, our sense of self, is at stake. Secularity is a way of being dependent on the responses of our milieu. The secular or false self is the self which is fabricated, as Thomas Merton says, by social compulsions. "Compulsive" is indeed the best adjective for the false self. It points to the need for ongoing and increasing affirmation. Who am I? I am the one who is liked, praised, admired, disliked, hated, or despised. Whether I am a pianist, a businessman or a minister, what matters is how I am perceived by the world.3

The drive to be liked or accepted drives us right into a trap. It's a cycle that includes engaging in an increasingly high amount of purposeful behavior intended to earn acceptance. The acceptance creates an even stronger dependence upon future acceptance. Then we work even harder to attain the acceptance we *need*. It works like a drug addiction. This is why the Bible says "the fear of man is a snare" (Proverbs 29:15). This cycle takes us further and further from our true identity. Eventually, there may be such a wide chasm between the false self and the true self that we don't know what's true and what's not. This is precisely why it's so important to allow God to reveal our true heart.

I think many people live in this place. There's an unexplainable sense that something is not quite right, but we keep plowing forward with life. We keep busy. We are driven to accomplish. We jump through the hoops in order to taste acceptance. For Manning, that meant studying hard, getting excellent grades, and so on. For me, that meant impressing people through athletic accomplishment, excelling at work, and more. These things are not bad in and of themselves, but they become dangerous when our motive for doing them is to prove our worth to others.

Remember that Satan tried to tempt Jesus to prove Himself. Jesus didn't engage in his game because He didn't need to prove Himself. His identity was secure. He knew He was the beloved Son and the delight of His Father. He heard the Father's affirmation before He performed any of His miracles and before He officially started His ministry. His ministry flowed from a secure heart that knew sonship. Jesus understood that there was nothing He could "do" to add value and worth to His life.

The same is true for you and me. Our value is exclusively found in the fact that we are deeply loved children of God. Don't race past this important truth. Anything that we try and do in an effort to add to our worth through work or performance feeds the false self and takes us further from the life of freedom.

THE FREEDOM TO BE YOU

Jesus lived with a fierce freedom. He lived from His heart. He loved deeply. He felt deep compassion for others. He was merciful. He wept. He grieved. He laughed. He turned the world upside down. He set the captives free.

He's still setting the captives free. He wants to set your heart free. He wants your heart to taste a glorious freedom. This is the gift that He wants to give you, which will also be a gift to the world. The greatest gift you can offer others is the real you.

I was huffing and puffing on a run recently, but I still heard the whisper of the Father over the clomping of my feet: *Gabe, this world would look so different if my people simply understood who they really are.* It was a powerful statement, but I also picked up on the personal invitation seeded in His words. It was an invitation John Eldredge describes this way: *"Come, and live out what I meant you to be."*4 God was drawing me deeper into my own heart. He was telling me that there was much more for me to discover about who He made me to be.

I responded to His invitation by making two different lists: "What Satan is saying about my life" and "What the Father is saying about my life." I asked the Father to reveal the lies I had believed about myself and started listing them in order. Then I started compiling a list of Bible verses on the topic of identity: "I am fearfully and wonderfully made" (Psalm 139), "I am a beloved child of God" (1 John 3:1), and more. After I filled my mind with Scripture, I started listening for the personal words of the Father. He loves to take the truth of Scripture and impart it in deeply personal ways to our hearts. One by one, He started speaking truth over me, and it was extremely refreshing. Then I placed these statements in a place where they would serve as a continual reminder of what the Father says about me. I also renounced the lies of the enemy and repented to the Father for believing them.

Finally, I wanted to share with my wife what I had heard the Father speak about me. I wanted to invite her to challenge me when she saw a discrepancy between my life and the words of the Father. In a sense, I was asking her to be a sort of "Rafiki." I approached her and said, "You're my baboon."

She gave me the look. It was a look with which I am quite familiar.

10.
BRAVE HEART

I understand that all this "find your heart" talk can lead some to think I'm advocating a life of self-absorption. Perhaps it sounds like I'm encouraging people to spend so much time in their internal world that they become ignorant of others. This couldn't be further from the truth.

When we discover our true heart, we'll discover our true identity. The revelation of our identity leads to a deeper understanding of our purpose. Our purpose is to love, and love is focused on others. Scripture makes it clear that our highest calling is to love God and love others (Matthew 22).

In other words, your identity should be rooted in the truth that you are the beloved. You are loved with a passionate and furious love, and this consuming love will compel you to love others. The apostle John, who actually referred to himself as the "beloved," declared: *We love because He first loved us* (1 John 4:19). Paul put it this way: *The love of Christ compels us . . .* (2 Corinthians 5:14). Our primary purpose is to receive and give the love of Jesus.

My false self knows nothing of this love. It's a life of shadows—there's an appearance but not substance. As Brennan Manning said: "It's a life that everyone will admire but nobody will know."[1] This projected image is designed to impress others in order to create a sense of worth and value. It's impossible for the false self to love because it doesn't know what it means to be loved. The Father isn't interested in loving the false self either; the Father wants to destroy the false self. This is because the false self is a thief—he robs me of the true joy of being loved by God, and he robs God of the glory that results from me genuinely living a life that bears His image.

My true heart desires to love because it knows great love. I can testify to the truth of the apostle John's words: *See what great love the Father has lavished on us, that we should be called children of God* (1 John 3:1, NIV). I once asked the Father to reveal what was true about my heart, and He said: *lover.* If this is the case, then my life is most congruent with the Master's original design when I love Him and love others.

Love can be tough. The sinful nature, the part of me that wants to be absorbed by me, raises its unsightly head and demands I get my way. I think I concede too often. With three kids under the age of five, my patience is tested on a regular basis. We had a moment a couple days ago when all three were screaming in unison. It sounded like a bad country and western song. It was the end of the day, and Ashley and I were exhausted. We looked at each other as if to say, *Do they sell one way tickets to the moon?*

Parenting was one of God's brilliant ideas. Not only does He place parents in a position to learn about His love as a Father, but He provides us with ample opportunity to put that love into practice on a daily basis. He generously extends continual invitations to crush every ounce of selfishness within us. Scrubbing the carpet at 3 a.m. after a child has projected vomit across their bedroom? Check. Changing diapers with a smell so bad it could wake the dead? Check. Telling kids to share their toys and stop fighting for the 973rd time today? Check. Trying to convince your teenager that you know better than them? Check. It's hard work, but it's absolutely beautiful. When we love, we live from our true heart. We become more of who we already are. We were created to live a life of love, so it's fair to say that we're not really living if we're not really loving.

It's also fair to say that love requires raw courage. Love originates from the heart, which means the heart is required to be present and vulnerable. When the heart is vulnerable, the possibility is there to experience intense pain. I think heart pain has to be the worst kind of pain. Slamming your finger in the car door or enduring a double root canal pales in comparison to the consistent ache that comes from a broken heart.

Having experienced deep pain in the heart makes me appreciate the courageous love of God. He put His heart on the line from day one. Watching His beloved creation, Adam and Eve, reject Him and choose their own path must have been utterly heartbreaking. The thing He desired the most—intimacy with His people—was gone in a second. The pain only intensified until we see the following appear in Genesis 6:

> *The LORD observed the extent of human wicked-ness on the earth, and he saw that everything they thought or imagined was consistently and totally evil. So the LORD was sorry he had ever made them and put them on the earth. It broke his heart.* (Genesis 6:5-6, NLT)

What a sad text of Scripture. Those are not just words on a page; the heart of God was actually filled with sear-ing pain. What's even more amazing is that He continued to keep His heart engaged. He didn't retreat and give up on mankind. So much of the Old Testament is the story of God being faithful to His people, even while His people pulled away and rejected Him. If you think this didn't af-fect the heart of a loving God, think again.

The Scriptures give us a glimpse into the heart of God in Jeremiah 2:

> *I remember how eager you were to please me*
> *as a young bride long ago,*
> *how you loved me and followed me*
> *even through the barren wilderness.*
> *In those days Israel was holy to the LORD,*
> *the first of his children.*
> *All who harmed his people were declared guilty,*
> *and disaster fell on them.* (Jeremiah 2:2-3, NLT)

There's a certain level of tenderness to this passage. God was recalling the *glory* days when His people were devoted to Him, when they loved Him. He could have written His own country and western song. He follows with an interesting question: *What did your ancestors find wrong with me that led them to stray so far from me?* (Jeremiah 2:5, NLT).

It was a legitimate question that revealed His true desire for intimacy. *Why don't you love me? What fault did you find in me? Why are you pulling away rather than leaning in?* He could have said: *"Listen you bunch of little punks! I loved you, but you rejected me. Prepare to die. I'm out."* Forget the country song, He could have produced a metal song. We're talking about rejection. Rejection is painful, and pain can easily turn to anger. It's hard to read the Bible and not see the anger of God in the Old Testament, but the amazing thing with God is what He does with anger—He takes it upon Himself. The wrath of God was placed upon Jesus as He bore the sin of the world on Calvary's cross. God simply never stopped loving. His heart never retreated.

God possesses an extraordinarily brave heart. The result of His audacious courage was victory. It was worth it in the end, because love conquered all. Love stared death in the face, and it was death that retreated. The song playing from heaven is not a dreary country song, nor is it an angry metal song. It's a song of joy and victory. It's a song of deep celebration.

It's a song that invites us to possess the same courage and taste of the same victory. It's a song that beckons us to live a life of love, even in the face of death. A song that continually reminds us of this prevailing truth:

Love never fails.

RESISTING FEAR

Love always wins, and perfect love always casts out fear (1 John 4:18). There is no fear in love, as the beloved apostle reminds us. You were designed to love, which means you were meant to be a deeply courageous person.

If God possesses a courageous heart, and you were created in His likeness, what does that mean about your true heart? You have an unending well of courage deep within you. Jesus, with all of His courage, resides in your heart. This is why one of the most frequent commands in Scripture is to *fear not.*

God has made it abundantly clear that He did not create you to be a fearful and timid person. Paul declares, *For God has not given us a spirit of fear and timidity, but of power, love, and self-discipline* (2 Timothy 1:7, NLT). The real version of you is overflowing with power and love. The Scripture also states: *So you have not received a spirit that makes you fearful slaves. Instead, you received God's Spirit when he adopted you as his own children. Now we call him, "Abba, Father." For his Spirit joins with our spirit to affirm that we are God's children* (Romans 8:15-16, NLT).

If we weren't created to be fearful slaves, then how does fear develop such a stronghold in our lives? One access point is through pain. We taste the bitterness of pain and decide we'll do anything to avoid experiencing it again. The heart is buried in order to protect itself, and the false self is created for self-protection.

The false self is timid and scared at its core—even if the projected image appears to be aggressive and bold.

I counseled one man who put up an extremely aggressive front—his family was scared of him—but deep down he was riddled with fear. He was a tall, seemingly powerful man, who was extremely blunt and direct. He looked hardened. When these layers were peeled back though, I saw what looked like a scared little boy.

The more we allow the false self to dominate, the more we welcome fear into our lives. The imposter is birthed from a place of fear, which means it will always be captive to fear. The way to rid your life of fear is by learning to live from your true heart. It's a process of learning to exercise the courage that you possess on a moment to moment basis. For many, this will feel like a really foreign and strange process.

Imagine a baby boy is born with healthy arms and legs, but is neglected and never taught to walk. He grows older and becomes a young toddler. Even though the boy has legs designed for walking, he still decides to crawl or sit rather than walk because this is what feels natural. The boy possesses everything needed to walk, but he has to learn how. He needs to be taught. He has to engage the process and exercise his legs until walking comes naturally. It may feel weird at first, but he'll eventually prefer walking to crawling.

The same is true with courage. We possess a spirit of boldness and power, but we have to engage the process of learning how to exercise it consistently. We need to be taught how to live courageously, and the Father is ready and willing to teach us. Eventually, the things that once scared us will seem laughable. This process unfolds on a daily basis as we're confronted with choices to step forward in courage or retreat in fear. We're either giving up ground or gaining ground every day. Any encounter with fear results in a retreat—either we'll retreat or fear will retreat.

I was enjoying a relaxing walk with my family recently when a little poodle came charging off its porch and headed straight for us. The little yapper didn't weigh an ounce over fifteen pounds—and it only had three legs—but it acted like a hungry lion that had just spotted its prey. Instead of retreating, I took one step towards the little dog, and it hit the brakes, turned around, and bolted. The dog suddenly had an epiphany as soon as it realized we weren't scared. If I would have retreated, the lopsided mutt would have chased us all the way home. Fear operates in the same manner. As we stand up to fear—resisting the devil in the power and authority of Jesus—he will be forced to flee (James 4:17). Sometimes the devil just really needs an epiphany of his own—a simple reminder that *greater is He who is in you than he who is in the world* (1 John 4:4, NASB).

We can provide this cordial reminder by refusing to retreat today. Over the next twenty-four hours, let's look for opportunities to strengthen our "courage" muscle. Then let's do it again tomorrow and the next day. The journey of taking back territory for the kingdom of God starts with the first step forward. Ask the Father to give you eyes to see what that step is today.

In addition, consider the following questions: What would your life look like if you didn't give place to fear? If you were strictly motivated by love, how different would your daily life be? Would you be pursuing some dreams that you're currently ignoring? Would you be more intentional in your pursuit of certain relationships? Would you take more risks? The answers to these questions may shed light on the dreams God has for your life (which is what we'll explore in the next chapter).

II.
FIELD OF DREAMS

Love is a courageous act. Living a life of hope is too. The Father designed us to be hopeful people. Our hearts are meant to be so filled with hope that they drip. In fact, hope is essential to victorious Christian living. Still, too few people are living hopeful lives. We have retreated and given up ground in this area of life, but it's time to change this. It's time to take another step forward.

I'm currently leaning back in my squeaky chair and looking out my second story office window. It's a great view that overlooks a local school's football field. Further up on the ridge is the western boundary of a partially scorched Black Forest. A little more than three months ago, I watched out this same window as helicopters armed with giant buckets tried desperately to squelch the horrifying flames that were roaring out of control in the forest, less than two miles from where I was sitting. It was a scene right out of a movie, and unfortunately, a scene right out of my memory.

Twelve months prior—almost exactly to the day—I watched as a different wildfire (the Waldo Canyon Fire) rudely barged into our city limits and wreaked a path of destruction that left hundreds of people without homes. It was a sight I had hoped I would never witness again, but sadly, my eyes viewed what seemed to be an instant replay from the previous year.

Today's window view is quite different. I just watched as a young boy (probably third grade), dressed in a red polo and tan khakis, ran with a football, dodged imaginary tacklers, and did a spin move into the end zone. He spiked the ball with as much strength as he could muster, and he lifted his arms in celebration as the imaginary crowd chanted his name. He thought nobody was looking, but I gave him a standing ovation from my office. It was, again, a scene right out of my memory.

Watching the young boy dream about making would be tacklers look foolish reminded me of my childhood. I would often ride my bike to the local football field, put on cleats that were two sizes too big, and pretend I was suddenly orchestrating a historic fourth quarter comeback. The 75,000 screaming Notre Dame fans were cheering me on, and so was "Touchdown Jesus."

I'm assuming khaki boy and me aren't the only two who have ever acted out such audacious dreams. I recently went on a run and saw a young boy playing basketball in his front driveway. He dribbled between his legs and attempted a turnaround buzzer beater, which he missed badly. He was quick to allow room in his imagination for one more second on the clock in order to sprint to the hoop and kiss the ball off the backboard for the *real* winning bucket. He too threw his arms in the air and celebrated—and then tried to act cool as he realized somebody had actually witnessed his heroics.

His dream wasn't about to end in failure. What kid dreams of coming up short? In my dreams, not once did I get tackled short of the goal line as time expired; neither did I see khaki boy get flattened by an imaginary Brian Urlacher. He scored every time, and he celebrated with vigor after every score.

Isn't it interesting that kids have a natural capacity to dream big? Not only do they dream, but they dream about victory and beauty. Little boys dream about being the hero and little girls dream about being the beautiful princess.

And then they grow up.

Don't get me wrong—adults still dream. We still harbor in our hearts a picture of what we think the future will look like, but the nature of the picture changes drastically as we get older. Beauty and victory often disappear, and instead, the colors become dark and dreary. It's almost as if the paintbrush changes hands and a new artist begins his work. Mark Twain once penned, "I have lived through some terrible things in my life, some of which actually happened."

Isn't this easy to allow? We buy into a picture of the future that gives far too much room for fear and worry. Somewhere along the way, we subconsciously ask the Master Artist to put down His paintbrush, and we allow the enemy to paint a *safer* picture that doesn't require faith or hope.

It feels safe because we all know that hope is risky business. Hope involves jostling your heart from its slumber and putting its neck on the line. And besides, this is hostile territory. Tragedy strikes. Houses burn. Jobs vanish. Relationships crumble. So do city walls.

NEHEMIAH'S DREAM

The Bible tells a story about a courageous man who carried a big dream in the midst of tragic circumstances. He refused to give up hope. Nehemiah heard the report that Jerusalem's walls had been broken down and its gates burned. When he heard the news, he sat down and wept for days. He mourned and fasted, and then he prayed and began to dream about rebuilding a wall and a city.

I'm intrigued by his ability to seek God's vision after such a tragic event. His heart didn't retreat to the basement of his soul. He was not about to allow the artist of destruction to paint the final picture in this story. This was not the time or place to retreat; this was a time to dream God's dreams, to let hope rise in his soul, and pursue those dreams with an unwavering passion and courage until they became reality. The kingdom of darkness trembles in the presence of such a soul, and the enemy actively works to diminish this hope and return the heart to its slumber.

Nehemiah experienced wave after wave of opposition. One of the primary tactics the enemy employed to oppose Nehemiah and attempt to diminish his hope and squash his dream was the ridiculing words of others.

Listen to Nehemiah's own words:

> When Sanballat heard that we were rebuild-
> ing the wall, he became angry and was greatly
> incensed. He ridiculed the Jews, and in the pres-
> ence of his associates and the army of Samaria,
> he said, "What are those feeble Jews doing? Will
> they restore their wall? Will they offer sacrifices?
> Will they finish in a day? Can they bring the stones
> back to life from those heaps of rubble—burned
> as they are?"
>
> Tobiah the Ammonite, who was at his side, said,
> "What they are building—even a fox climbing up
> on it would break down their wall of stones!"
> (Nehemiah 4:1-3, NIV)

The answer was yes. God certainly did bring the
"stones back to life from those heaps of rubble." He created beauty from ashes through the faithfulness and
obedience of Nehemiah and the Jews he had inspired.
The wall was rebuilt and hope was restored—even in
hostile territory.

God is still doing this today. He's creating rivers of
hope in a dry and barren land. He's urging us to "forget the former things; do not dwell on the past" (Isaiah
43:18). Why? Because He's doing a new thing. As the
prophet Isaiah wrote:

> See, I am doing a new thing!
> Now it springs up; do you not perceive it?
> I am making a way in the wilderness
> and streams in the wasteland. (Isaiah 43:19, NIV)

He's erasing the dreary painting of the enemy and creating something much more spectacular. He knows the plans He has for you, and they are plans for hope and a future. They aren't plans to simply help you keep your head above water or barely make life work. They are victorious, beautiful, and glorious plans, and God is passionate about making them a reality in your life. As we allow God's dreams to become our dreams, we will experience the arrival of hope and passion; perhaps the kind of passion that once resided in us as kids.

Why shouldn't we recover our ability to dream hopeful dreams; dreams of victory and beauty? I'm not advocating a life of fantasy, but I'm saying the picture we hold of our future shouldn't be full of anxiety, fear, and dread. Hope should be one of the defining characteristics of our lives as Christians. The tomb was empty on the third day! The one who sits enthroned over all things is the one who is for you.

Hope rises as we allow our hearts to be the field in which God plants the seeds of His dreams. I guarantee the dreams the Father has for you are victorious. They're dreams of you loving Him and His people, building His kingdom, and producing fruit at every turn. He dreams of you living a powerful, joyful, and peaceful life. He dreams of your heart being whole and holy before Him.

One of the reasons our hearts may not be *whole* and healthy is because we lack real hope. The Scripture says, "Hope deferred makes the heart sick" (Proverbs 13:12, NIV). The Bible also explains that "a cheerful heart is good medicine" (Proverbs 17:22, NIV). The Father wants you to dream with Him, to hope with Him, and as a result, to laugh with Him as the dreams become reality.

This isn't meant to be theory, but God wants to see this become a reality for your heart. A possible starting place is to carve out time in the next week specifically designed for dreaming with God. I encourage you to create a sort of "bucket list" with Him. Ask the Father to show you what He dreams of for your life. What are things that He wants to do with you this year? How about the next five or ten years? Remember the words you heard Him speak over your life from a previous chapter? Allow Him to expand those words and paint an even clearer picture.

I just started praying this over my own life. I was asking for the dreams of the Father to be the same dreams that reside in my heart. I started creating my own bucket list with Him. The first thing I noticed was that God's dreams are much bigger than mine. *Really, God? You want me to do that?* I thought about dismissing it, but then He reminded me about the previous chapter and the importance of courage.

As I prayed, my eyes naturally shifted from my computer screen to the window again. The clouds are hanging over the ridge in a way that is eerily similar to the smoke plumes from last summer. If I squint, I can even see the torched trees that remain. An ugly reminder of reality.

However, I can also see the field.

A reminder to dream anyway.

12.
MUCH NEEDED SNOW

From New Life Church, the Black Forest burn scar is evident by looking to the east. The Waldo Canyon burn scar can be seen by looking to the west. Both directions contain views of trees that look like splintered toothpicks and blackened soil that looks like its been carted in from the deepest regions of hell. I recently stood in the World Prayer Center (a beautiful prayer facility on the campus of New Life with huge windows looking west, overlooking Pikes Peak and the front range of the Rocky Mountains) and watched the sun slowly rise and cast its beautiful light upon Rampart Range.

Very little snow was visible to the right or left of the burn area on the mountain, but the scar itself had a layer of snow resting upon it. The snow looked like medicine from heaven covering the scorched earth, making the blackened soil appear beautiful. It was literally beauty from ashes.

The snow on the burn scar was a powerful visual of what God desires to do in our lives. He desires to place a layer of fresh snow on our scars! He wants to place His healing medicine on the parts of our hearts that have been burned. As I stood and enjoyed the powerful visual, the Father spoke: *This is what I want to do. I want my love, kindness, grace, and healing to rest upon the scars of My people. I want to heal their hearts.*

God always has been and always will be a healer. He's in the business of binding up the brokenhearted, proclaiming liberty to captives, comforting those who mourn, and creating beauty from ashes (Isaiah 61).

He's worked wonders in my heart, and I'm deeply grateful for the healing I've experienced, but I also believe He's not done. In fact, I woke up at 4 a.m. a few weeks ago, after having a dream that stirred up some pain from my past. It was as if God was shining a spotlight on that particular area of my heart. The invitation was, *Will you allow me to bring snow to this area of your heart?* The pain was nearly suffocating, but I knew better than to run from the only one who can make me whole.

When we experience pain, the last thing we want to do is allow anyone near it—including God. Our initial reaction is to bury it and hope it goes away. As nice as that would be, it's simply not reality. Our buried pain quickly works against us as it eventually hardens our hearts and makes us numb in certain areas. Unaddressed pain also creates a scenario where people often adopt dysfunctional behaviors simply because they are acting out their stifled emotions. This can lead to heavy chains of addiction and a plethora of other negative possibilities. It's easier said than done, but a much better option is to allow God to deal with our hurt. That process can start with the following question: *Father, is there any unresolved pain in my heart that needs attention?*

One of the mistakes we make is to think we are responsible for our own healing. God's responsibility is to create beauty from ashes. Our responsibility is to keep the door open to Him. One lady sat in my office and said, "I've dealt with this pain for fifty years. Will it ever go away?" The more we explored the cause for the lingering pain, the more the answer became increasingly evident. She finally admitted that she often asks God to heal her heart, but she also takes control back before He's allowed to work. She invites Him to work, but then she slams the door on Him and returns to what is comfortable.

The idea of keeping our heart open to Jesus is crucial to the healing process. When we invite Him, He literally comes. It's too easy to turn Jesus into a theory or idea, but the same Jesus who placed His healing hands on the hurting over two thousand years ago desires to come and place His pierced hands on our pain. The result will be wholeness and healing. This is not a theory or mere fancy sounding idea, it's a deep spiritual reality. It's the hope we have in life.

Her eyes brightened and a look of relief appeared upon her face as I said, "Let me give you a simple challenge: Keep the door of your heart open to God. Let Him bring the healing *snow*." It may sound overly simplistic, but doesn't the problem often lie in the fact that we try and take control of our own healing? We think we can make it on our own, but we end up like the bird stuck in my garage—the pain is only prolonged. There is freedom in allowing God to do what He desires to do. He's the expert Physician, and He knows exactly what your heart needs.

THE UNIQUENESS OF THE HEALING PROCESS

It's also important to remember the healing process won't necessarily look the same for each person. There is an element of human nature where we want a formula. We want the map before we set out on the journey.

One morning, I had coffee with a friend who was facing some major life decisions. He said, "I just wish God would give me point A, B, C, and D. Then I would know exactly what He was after." I laughed out loud and said, "Yeah, me too. But then I'm pretty sure I'd leave Him in the dust."

The healing process works in a similar fashion. If healing required simply following a formula that was the same for everyone, we would eventually revert to taking control of our own healing. It would be a clean, safe, and easily controlled process where we knew exactly what to expect at each point. And we would forfeit the true intimacy with Jesus which actually creates an environment for the healing to occur.

John Eldredge captures it well, writing:

If you wanted to learn how to heal the blind and you thought that following Christ around and watching how he did it would make things clear, you'd wind up pretty frustrated. He never does it the same way twice. He spits on one guy, for another, he spits on the ground and makes mud and puts that on his eyes. To a third he simply speaks, a fourth he touches, and a fifth he kicks out a demon. There are no formulas with God. The way in which God heals our wound is a deeply personal process.[1]

Your pain probably didn't occur in the same manner as your neighbor's pain, so the healing process needs to be unique and personal to you. Jesus will come to heal your pain in the perfect manner in the perfect timing. While it's a unique and personal process, there are a few things we can do to cooperate with Him.

COOPERATING WITH THE PROCESS

First, we must be authentic and honest regarding the condition of our heart. Is your heart fully alive? Are you experiencing the *joy that knows no bounds*? Do you have a *peace that surpasses understanding?* Do you love deeply and allow yourself to be moved by the things that move God? Are you compassionate towards others? Are you quick to offer mercy? These are good questions to ask to get a guage on the current condition of your heart.

I've never met a single person who didn't need a little heart work. Life is messy—even violent so at times. The heart suffers pain as a result of living in a broken world. The key is to pay attention to the *dashboard lights* and understand when we need to allow Jesus to provide heart healing.

My car started sounding funny a few months ago. The "check engine" light came on, confirming my notion that something wasn't right under the hood. At the same time, I didn't want to check under the hood, because I was afraid I would find something seriously wrong. Not only would this be an inconvenience to my schedule, but it would also mean coughing up the hundreds of dollars needed to make things right. I tried to play the ignorance card for a few more days, but I realized I was probably just making it worse. Only after I decided to stop ignoring the problem and took it to the shop for repair did it start running like new again.

I think many people are afraid of taking an honest look at their hearts because they're afraid of what they'll find. If something does need attention, it would surely be a horrible inconvenience, right? Many would rather live the next fifty years with a dull heart than carve out some time in this current season to intentionally pursue healing and wholeness. If you're waiting for the ideal time, you'll be waiting for the rest of your life. Life won't slow down anytime soon. The reality is that the longer we ignore the issue, the worse it will become.

But, it's so scary to even go there. It's so personal. I've heard these statements many times as people consider moving in the direction of healing. It sounds like a good idea until Jesus starts moving close. Then it becomes extremely real and people often get squirmy. I understand how difficult this can be, but remember, you were created for wholeness. The degree of richness you experience in life is correlated to the degree in which your heart is healthy. As Proverbs 4 reminds us, life flows from the heart. I started this book with the invitation for you to go deeper with God, and His beckoning call is still sounding. He has more for your life!

This is a serious topic, and it's helpful to have people walk alongside us on the healing journey. We are the most vulnerable when we are alone and isolated. When we engage something so important as the healing of our heart, we need to be in trusted community. I encourage you to be intentional, to really pray about the right people to invite alongside you. You'll need prayer. Like Moses, you'll need others to *lift your arms* when you're feeling weak. This may include a pastor or a professional counselor. Just don't try and go at it alone. Be courageous in the process of developing community.

Finally, give yourself permission to grieve. This is sometimes uncomfortable, but it's incredibly healthy for the heart. It allows you to deal with the pain rather than leave it buried. This is not a sign of weakness but of incredible strength. David, the warrior king who slayed the mighty giant, was a man familiar with grieving. After Saul died, *David and all the men with him took hold of their clothes and tore them. They mourned and wept and fasted till evening for Saul and his son Jonathan, and for the army of the LORD and for the nation of Israel, because they had fallen by the sword* (2 Samuel 1:11-12, NIV).

We must not forget about Jesus. After learning of Lazarus' death, *Jesus wept.* This is interesting because a few verses later, we see Jesus bringing Lazarus back to life. He could have easily bypassed the grieving process and cut straight to the chase, the resurrection of His friend. He wasn't in a hurry. He allowed Himself to experience the pain of the moment. He modeled grieving for us. Jesus' grief reveals how healthy His heart really was. He allowed Himself to experience and express His emotions.

MOVING TOWARDS HEALING

Take a few deep breaths and calm your mind. Remember that the Father loves you more than you can even fathom. He created you for freedom, life, and wholeness. He is light and He is love. He has your absolute best in mind. Now ask Him to reveal the condition of your heart. Ask Him if there is a part of your heart that needs healing.

Take your time with this question. Be fully present with Him. There is nothing more valuable to Him than your heart. What you're doing is courageous and important.

Ask Him to give you a picture that represents the current condition of your heart. Remember that visuals are powerful communication tools—for example, the burn scar on the mountain. Give Him the opportunity to bring something to your mind or heart. It may be a picture you see in your spirit, or it may be something that you see with your physical eyes today or later this week.

In addition, ask Him to give you a picture that represents the condition of your heart after healing. It may be the freedom of the blue sky, or the calm waters of a pond or lake, but give Him the opportunity to reveal His intentions. One person asked this question and then looked up to see the American flag blowing proudly in the wind. The flag represents the glorious freedom we experience as Americans, and the Father was essentially communicating that His desire was for this person to experience an even deeper level of glorious freedom in their heart.

Lastly, ask Him who you should invite to walk with you on this journey. Who has He called to love you, pray for you, and offer strength and encouragement? Remember this is a process. Just be committed to taking one step at a time on the path to wholeness. The first step can even be this prayer:

Father, I believe you created me for wholeness. Today, I'm choosing wholeness. I realize this will be a process, but I ask for the courage to move forward towards healing. I trust you. I open my heart to you and ask you to bring your healing "snow" upon my heart. Let my heart be the canvas in which you create beauty from ashes. Thank you. Thank you. Thank you. In Jesus Name. Amen.

13.
BOLTED SHUT

One significant way to cooperate with God in the healing process is through forgiveness. This is one of the healthiest gifts you can ever give your heart, and it does a great deal to facilitate healing and wholeness. Remember how important it is to keep the door open to Jesus throughout the healing process? It's also important to keep the door closed to the enemy. That sounds almost too obvious to even state, but he's a stealthy little creature. He can be a sly fox. He's crouching at the door and we often don't recognize how he's trying to gain entry.

The Scripture states: *Above all else, guard your heart, for everything you do flows from it* (Proverbs 4:23, NIV). Guarding our hearts requires a high level of attentiveness and intentionality. We have to be fierce, even if it means showing our teeth.

One of my old dogs was quite possibly the nicest dog that's ever lived. She wouldn't have hurt a fly. However, if you gave her a leftover steak bone, she turned into a completely different animal. She would take the bone and position herself in the far corner of the yard. She would establish an invisible fence and make it abundantly clear that you better keep your distance while she savored the rare treat. If you came within ten feet, she would sound a monstrous growl while flashing her threatening teeth. If you didn't regard her warning, you'd most likely end up with missing fingers. She was committed to guarding that bone. What would happen if we were as passionate about guarding our hearts? Aren't our hearts more valuable than a hardened and previously chewed steak bone?

If we valued our hearts even half as much as God values them, we would be a lot better at keeping the door bolted shut to the enemy.

DON'T OPEN THE DOOR

In elementary school I had a friend named Travis. One day, Travis and I were alone in his house. It was early evening, but still plenty dark as the two of us played video games in his living room. At one point, he looked up from the game and with a startled look in his eyes, asked, "Did you hear that?"

A few moments later, I heard a scratching noise that appeared to be coming from outside his kitchen window. Then we heard the sound of shuffling feet on his back patio, followed by a loud thump. My thumper nearly jumped out of my chest as we listened to someone trying to force their way in through the back door.

"Go get the phone!" I said with sheer panic in my voice. He looked just as scared, and replied, "The phone is by the back door. No way!"

Our terror grew as we heard the front screen door open and the person now trying to force their way in through that door. We ran for a nearby closet, hid ourselves in utter darkness, and listened to the pounding on the door and the pounding in our chests—I'm not sure which was louder. Neither one of us knew what to do, but we were smart enough to know that we shouldn't open the door and invite the intruder in.

I wish I would have applied the same logic to the spiritual thief during my dark years in college. My thinking during those years was essentially that it was OK to allow the thief to enter my heart as long as he agreed to stay in the basement. In other words, I kept participating in my favorite sinful behaviors, but I would stay away from more "serious" sin. I failed to realize that the devil creates a stronghold by first establishing a foothold. As the old saying goes, sin always takes us further than we want to go and keeps us longer than we want to stay. I shouldn't have been surprised when things came up missing—my joy, peace, healthy relationships, and aspects of my health. I allowed the thief access, and he proceeded to steal.

That season taught me a great deal about the importance of guarding my heart. I am more committed than ever to watching closely over my life. There's too much at stake. When I feel the tug of temptation, I often picture a thief trying to break through a door. It helps solidify a position of resistance.

One of the most common ways the enemy gains access to someone's heart is through unforgiveness and bitterness. A person is most susceptible to the dangers of unforgiveness after being hurt. The pain often makes it hard to recognize the *knocking of the thief* as he attempts to enter and make himself at home. It's much more common to focus our attention on the person who caused the pain.

This is a dangerous scenario, primarily because the enemy remains undetected. It's a classic *bait and switch.* He tries to get our attention focused on the person who caused the pain, and then he enters through the cracked door when we're not looking. Once he enters, he works to fuel our anger in an effort to slide into an even more subtle and hidden position. The more we focus on the offense, the less we notice the true perpetrator.

Recall the words of the apostle Paul: *For we are not fighting against flesh-and-blood enemies, but against evil rulers and authorities of the unseen world, against mighty powers in this dark world, and against evil spirits in the heavenly place*s (Ephesians 6:12, NLT).

Darkness in this world is easy to see, but it's also hard to see. We recognize when a violation has taken place, but we don't always see the one ultimately behind the violation. An important component in guarding our hearts from bitterness is correctly identifying the original thief and violator—Satan.

Satan is coming against you in a variety of ways, one of which is through the words and actions of others. He works to develop a stronghold in a person's life, and then he uses that position to blind them and influence their behavior. The stronger the stronghold, the more hardened and blinded a person is to the truth.

I'm not excusing the actions and words of others, but I'm trying to provide some context for what may be happening behind the scenes. There's a strong possibility that in their heart, the person who offended you or hurt you has given up significant ground to the enemy. The devil quite possibly caused great pain in their life, and then entered through the open door of bitterness and unforgiveness. (He doesn't have new tricks.) How many times have we heard the saying: *Hurt people hurt people?* Don't allow this cycle to continue. Don't allow the enemy to take any more ground.

It's easier to keep the door of your heart closed to the enticing temptation of bitterness by remembering that God is a God of justice. Nothing escapes His sight. It is God's job to hold the violator accountable, and it's our job to trust that He will. He loves them way too much to not deal with them. If they continually refuse His love and correction, they'll have to give account on Judgment Day. Forgiveness is not ignoring the act and pretending like nothing happened, but rather releasing the violator into the reliable hands of God.

It's also important to note that forgiveness doesn't automatically equal trust. If you've been hurt, the violator has probably lost your trust. Offering forgiveness is very different from affording someone your full trust. Part of the process of guarding your heart might include guarding your heart from the person who hurt you! This requires discernment and the Father will extend wisdom to you in each unique situation.

Most importantly, remember the great cost required to purchase your forgiveness. You have been forgiven and set free of all your iniquity and depravity through the unimaginable sacrifice of Christ. The more the depth of this truth settles into the depth of your heart, the more you'll be inspired to offer forgiveness to others (at the same time, forgiveness is a choice rather than an inspirational feeling!). The Scripture commands us to forgive others, just as we've been forgiven (Ephesians 4:32). Jesus cast light on the seriousness of this topic by telling a short story:

> Therefore, the Kingdom of Heaven can be compared to a king who decided to bring his accounts up to date with servants who had borrowed money from him. In the process, one of his debtors was brought in who owed him millions of dollars. He couldn't pay, so his master ordered that he be sold—along with his wife, his children, and everything he owned—to pay the debt.
>
> But the man fell down before his master and begged him, "Please, be patient with me, and I will pay it all." Then his master was filled with pity for him, and he released him and forgave his debt.
>
> But when the man left the king, he went to a fellow servant who owed him a few thousand dollars. He grabbed him by the throat and demanded instant payment.
>
> His fellow servant fell down before him and begged for a little more time. "Be patient with me, and I will pay it," he pleaded. But his creditor wouldn't wait. He had the man arrested and put in prison until the debt could be paid in full.
>
> When some of the other servants saw this, they

were very upset. They went to the king and told him everything that had happened. Then the king called in the man he had forgiven and said, "You evil servant! I forgave you that tremendous debt because you pleaded with me. Shouldn't you have mercy on your fellow servant, just as I had mercy on you?" Then the angry king sent the man to prison to be tortured until he had paid his entire debt.

*That's what my heavenly Father will do to you if you refuse to forgive your brothers and sisters from your heart. (*Matthew 18:23-35, NLT)

The only thing more dangerous than allowing the enemy to enter our hearts through unforgiveness is facing a holy God after we've refused to forgive. The Bible explains that we'll all stand before God and give an account of our lives. It's far better to approach that day without a hint of bitterness in our hearts, rather than trying to offer up excuses for our unforgiving hearts to a deeply forgiving God.

It's simply best to settle the issue ahead of time. Let's be people who decide to forgive before the offense even happens. We live in a dark world, and it will only be a matter of time before someone does or says something to us that is hurtful. As you decide in advance to be a person of forgiveness, you're essentially establishing dead bolt locks on the door of your heart. You're preparing yourself for the inevitable knocking of the thief.

I was certainly glad we already had the locks in place before the intruder tried to enter Travis's house that night as we were gaming. The knocking and attempts at forced entry continued for five terrifying minutes before the person realized the locks were solid. The person eventually gave up and left, which also happens in the spiritual realm as we resist the evil one (James 4:7).

After we determined it was safe to come out of hiding, we slowly emerged from the darkness of the closet and peered down the long hallway leading to the living room. Then we heard another knock. My heart instantly returned to its previous location—in my throat—but then we heard the comforting sound of my parents' voices. They sounded like a heavenly choir. A flood of relief swept over us as we realized we were now safe.

We rushed over and opened the door, still visibly shaking, and detailed the trauma we had just experienced. My mom said, "Scott!"—as if to indicate she knew precisely who was behind this. It turns out it was my brother and his buddy playing a joke on us.

Real funny.

TWO POWERFUL WORDS

I certainly wasn't laughing as I stood with the phone pinned against my ear, waiting for what I knew would be a very uncomfortable and awkward conversation. I initially hoped the man I was calling wouldn't answer, but then I reminded myself that he needed to answer because I needed to repent.

A few mornings earlier, I was sitting on a balcony in Breckenridge, Colorado, overlooking a ski slope covered in snow that glistened in the Colorado sun. It was a beautiful sight, and my heart smiled as I reflected upon the goodness of God. The smile faded as

God surprised me with a very interesting topic of conversation. He brought to my mind memories of a person I had mistreated twenty years earlier, a victim of my childhood drive to be the ringleader and keep certain people out of the inner circle of popularity. I had spoken some cruel words against this particular person, and I had actively worked to turn others against him. It was all based in fear, but it still wasn't an excuse. God spoke to my heart and said: *I want you to call him and apologize.*

I hadn't seen, talked to, or even thought about this person in years, and God was asking me to call him out of the blue and apologize? I sipped my coffee and pondered what I was being asked to do. As much as I didn't feel like subjecting myself to what I thought would be a painfully awkward couple of minutes, I also reminded myself that obedience is always the best path. Plus, my heart was very different now and I did desire to make things right.

He picked up the phone, and with a much deeper voice than I remembered him having at age ten, said, "Hello?"

"Ummm, hi," I stammered as my heart was once again in my throat. "This is Gabe Jenkins. How are you?"

He politely engaged my attempt at small talk—I was stalling like crazy—and then I finally said: "I really called to apologize for the way I treated you when we were kids. I was wrong for acting the way I did. Will you forgive me?"

He was more than gracious, and he said, "I appreciate you calling, and I do forgive you." I could sense something heavy lift from him. I don't know the extent of the bitterness he may have carried against me due to the pain of rejection, but I know the call was significant for him. We eventually carried on with a normal conversation and shared what was happening in our lives. Perhaps he was internally shocked that a mean little brat grew up to be a pastor.

Extending forgiveness can be quite hard, but asking for forgiveness can be equally challenging. They are both important ingredients to a healthy heart, and they are each important to God. Jesus was delivering His infamous Sermon on the Mount when He commanded:

So if you are presenting a sacrifice at the altar in the Temple and you suddenly remember that someone has something against you, leave your sacrifice there at the altar. Go and be reconciled to that person. Then come and offer your sacrifice to God. (Matthew 5:23-24, NLT)

Two of the most powerful words in the English language are, "I'm sorry." Those seven letters have the capacity to create reconciliation, unity, and peace in our relationships. They can also bring us back into agreement with God when we sin against Him. I actually can't think of a single reason why we shouldn't be quick to repent. Sure our pride may take a hit, but isn't that a good thing? Not only does repentance help our hearts remain soft, but it also does a great deal to help others maintain a soft heart. If you offend someone, the enemy will try and seize the opportunity by knocking on the door of their heart, while offering them a neatly wrapped bouquet of bitterness. You can cut the enemy off at the knees by simply repenting to the person. As the Scripture says, love "always protects" (1 Corinthians 13:7). You are helping the person protect their heart from the deadly trap of unforgiveness. This is a courageous act of love done in humility, and it's deeply pleasing to the Father.

I encourage you to pause and reflect upon the importance of forgiveness and how it relates to your life. Do you think there's a possibility God is asking you to forgive someone? Is there someone who needs to hear an apology from you? I know it's not easy, but I also want to remind you of something important: You chose not to be a spectator in life. (Right?) If you're still reading, you are among the brave souls who refused to settle for beach life. Spectators would read a chapter like this and hurry along to the next. That's simply not beneficial.

Instead, allow the light of Jesus to descend into the deeper water of your heart. Give Him permission to reveal any hidden bitterness and unforgiveness that may be lurking below. If He reveals something, it's because He's after your healing and wholeness. Aggressively pursue the removal of that life-sucking cancer called bitterness.

One of the best ways to grab bitterness by the scruff of the neck and mercilessly eject it from your heart is to begin to genuinely pray for the person who hurt or offended you. While it's true that God doesn't like what they've done, He does love them with the same passion that He loves you. He wants to take back ground in their heart that they may have forfeited to the enemy. He wants to see them whole and holy. And He wants to use your prayers to help facilitate this process—both for their healing and for yours.

Father, I pray for ____ . What they did caused me pain, but I know you are my healer. I invite your healing into my heart. I forgive ____ and release them into your hands. You are a faithful and just God, and you will take care of this situation as you see fit. I bless ___ and pray for your kingdom to come and your will to be done in their life. I pray that you would open their eyes and show them your great love. Soften their heart today and show them the areas of their life where they have opened the door to the enemy. Father, give me the wisdom to know what my relationship should look like with ____ , moving forward. Thank you for loving me and for loving them. You are truly a great and awesome Father. In the name of Jesus, I pray. Amen.

The removal of bitterness from your heart only creates room for increased joy. One of the ways God brings joy into our lives is through the fulfillment of our deep desires. The next chapter explores the desires God has planted in the deep water of your heart and His unending passion to fulfill them.

14.
BORN TO RUN

Secretariat was a spectacular horse. "Big Red," as he was affectionately nicknamed, captured the hearts of millions of Americans en route to winning the Triple Crown in 1973. He was truly a horse designed to run, and run he did. What a glorious sight to see his ears laid back, a look of fiery determination in his eyes, and big powerful legs propelling him forward at a speed that left spectators speechless. People were in awe as they watched him run, and sometimes they responded in ways that didn't necessarily make sense to them. In the book, *The Horse God Built,* Lawrence Scanlan writes:

> Jack Nicklaus, the great golfer, was watching the Belmont Stakes at home. He ended up on all fours on his den floor, pounding on the floor, as this horse turned for home. Friends looking on were perplexed or aghast, or both. He said, "I don't know anything about horse racing, but for some reason I was pounding on the floor and tears were coming down."[1]

Scanlan also tells the story of Pete Rozelle, a very distinguished man who also happened to be the commissioner of the NFL at the time, standing on a table and cheering wildly as he watched the great horse run. It was very much out of character for Rozelle, but he couldn't help himself.

My favorite Secretariat story is said to have happened in that same race at Belmont, as he made a run at history. People were shocked at the blazing pace he maintained down the backstretch, and many questioned the sanity of the jockey, Ron Turcotte. They thought he was running Big Red into the ground, and they feared the sight of seeing the glorious horse collapse and literally die on the homestretch.

Scanlan writes:

What Ron Turcotte heard as he headed for the finish line that day in June of 1973 was an almost surreal quiet—just his horse's breathing and the drumming of his hooves. There was another sound, that of bedlam in the stands as the rafters shook, but Turcotte said it sounded like ocean surf to someone walking just out of sight of the sea. At the mile-and-an-eighth pole, the jockey heard a voice at the hedge yelling, "Ron, go on with that horse!" But when Turcotte looked, there was no one there. "I think" Nack told us, "Ronnie assumed it was God . . ."[2]

I wouldn't be surprised at all if God had been behind the mystery voice. I can picture God saying, "Watch this . . . I'm going to show the world what I've placed in this horse. Run, Red, Run . . ." Another man who was in the stands at Belmont said, "It looked like the Lord Himself held the reigns to that horse, like he bent over and whispered into his ear, 'Run . . .'"

God created a special horse, and God was glorified when that horse ran. Running was Secretariat's sweet spot, the very thing he was born to do. He oozed freedom, grace, and power as his ripped legs thrust him forward. Some cried, some danced on tables, some were left without words, but everyone took notice. They were witnessing greatness; they were watching a created being do exactly what it was created to do.

It's always a glorious sight to watch God's creation operate in its designed purpose—especially when that sight includes you. I can't help but think you and I carry a greater capacity to glorify God than even the most incredible horse. We are the ones He's labeled His "masterpiece." We are the ones who have been crafted and designed according to His glorious image. He has filled you with gifting and talents, and He wants to show the world what He's planted within you. He wants to hold the reigns and whisper, "Run!"

So what does this look like for your life? What is your sweet spot, the thing you were uniquely created to do to bring God glory? The answer lies deep within your heart, in the desires God has woven into your being. As we discover our true, God-planted desires we'll be moving in the direction of our calling.

I once heard a wise man say: "Your calling is the intersection where the deepest desires of your heart, your truest gifting, and the world's greatest need intersect." This is the bull's-eye for your life. This is the place where

God is calling you to really *run*. For me, I have a deep desire to write, broadcast, and counsel. The corresponding gifting God has given me is communication. The world's greatest need, as I see it, is for people to understand the deep goodness of God. When I'm writing, broadcasting, or counseling in regards to the goodness of God, I'm operating in my sweet spot—my unique calling.

It felt like I stumbled upon this calling, but that's not true. The more I think about it, the more I realize that I've carried these desires for years. Even as a young boy, I was intrigued by the idea of broadcasting and writing. I would turn my bedroom into a radio studio and broadcast to the world through a drumstick. Radio broadcasting moved my heart at a young age, which is why I'm not surprised that God opened doors later in life for me to enter the radio industry and broadcast His name. I also remember being a young boy and desiring to write about God. I even attempted to write a book when I was eight, but then I realized how much work was involved with a book endeavor and I put the project on hold for about twenty-four years. Looking back, there was great significance to the things that moved my heart at a young age.

A great place to begin the exploration of your desires is to ask yourself what moves your heart. As John Eldredge writes: "What makes you come alive? What stirs your heart? The journey we face now is into a land foreign to most of us. We must head into country that has no clear trail. This charter for exploration takes us into our own hearts, into our deepest desires."[3]

This journey requires intentionality and discipline. We live in a culture that tries to drag us along and force us to cave to its frenzied and hurried pace. There's little time to allow Jesus to reveal the desires that have been strategically placed in the deep water of our hearts. We have appointments to get to, bills to pay, soccer games to attend, projects to finish, and so on. The desires of the heart are often neglected and left to wither. It's a tragic mistake.

Dangerous Christians are those who create time and space in their lives to allow Jesus to excavate the desires He's planted within them, and then allow God to fulfill those desires for the express purpose of His glory. The more we allow Jesus to reveal and fulfill the desires of our heart, the more we'll come alive. As the Scriptures say, "a longing fulfilled is a tree of life" (Proverbs 13:12). The more alive we are, the more we'll glorify God. St. Iraneus said, "The glory of God is man fully alive."

Yes, I want that. But how does it happen? The way we allow Jesus to reveal and fulfill our true desires is found in a most intriguing verse: *Delight yourself in the Lord; And He will give you the desires of your heart* (Psalm 37:4, NASB). It's His primary responsibility to fulfill your desires in the right timing, and your primary responsibility to wholeheartedly engage Him in worship (delighting yourself in the Lord). I'm not just referring to worship as the songs you sing at church, but rather worship as a lifestyle. It's a life offered to God, a life lived in wonder and awe of who He is. The true desires of our heart will begin to surface in time as we consistently delight in Him. Worship acts as a refining fire that solidifies godly desire and loosens the grip of our carnal and sinful desire.

We've all experienced the tug of our sinful desires, the desires of the flesh. Nobody is exempt from these desires because we were born into a sinful world. The apostle Paul explains, *When you follow the desires of your sinful nature, the results are very clear: sexual immorality, impurity, lustful pleasures, idolatry, sorcery, hostility, quarreling, jealousy, outbursts of anger, selfish ambition, dissension, division, envy, drunkenness, wild parties, and other sins like these* (Galatians 5:19-21, NLT). On the other hand, Paul explains that the Spirit desires to produce the "fruit of the Spirit" within us: "love, joy, peace, patience, kindness, goodness, faithfulness, gentleness, and self-control." The desires of the flesh are in direct conflict with the desires of the Spirit, and the battleground in which this war rages on is within us.

Think of it as two completely different appetites. The appetite (desire) of our true heart craves the things of God. The appetite of our sinful nature craves the things of the world. We get to choose which appetite we satisfy, and we typically hunger for the things we feed upon most. I've gone through seasons where I've been a very healthy eater. I found that the more I ate healthy foods, the more my appetite longed for them. At other times, I've been an unhealthy eater, and it was during these seasons that my appetite craved *junk*. My appetite followed my eating decisions, and then my eating decisions followed my appetite. Like a snowball rolling down the hill, we can feed and strengthen our spiritual appetite or our carnal appetite by what we feed upon. For example, the more we spend countless hours perched in front of the television set or computer screen engrossed in the things of the world, the less we'll crave and desire the things of the Lord.

I think this is why the Scripture highlights the importance of "delighting yourself in the Lord" before God promises to fulfill your desires. He wants to strengthen your spiritual appetite so He can fulfill your God-given desires.

It's also important to note that the Scripture acts as a sword that separates godly desires from carnal desires. If you're unsure of the origin of a specific desire, turn to the truth of Scripture. God is not calling you to leave your spouse for another person, no matter how strong that desire may appear to be. There's no question this specific desire is of the flesh because the Scripture clearly commands us to be faithful to our spouse. The same process of discernment can be applied to a multitude of desires.

RETURNING TO THE QUESTION

With an understanding of the importance of worship and Scripture, let's return again to the question: What makes you come alive? Ask God to take you deep into your heart and reveal the desires He's given you. What were the things that moved you at a young age? What were the dreams you harbored as a young boy or girl? I've found that many people were more in tune with their God-given desires as a young child. Somewhere along the way the heart—with its desires—was buried and forgotten. It was pushed aside to make room for "reality."

Ask God if He wants to remind you of a specific passion you carried during your younger years that you've forgotten about. Ask Him if there's anything He wants to reignite. Pay more attention to the desire behind the childhood dream rather than the specifics of it. For example, I had a desire to start a grocery store in our local community when I was about seven. I obviously wasn't ready to open an actual store, but the true desire behind the dream was to be an entrepreneur and start something from scratch. This desire has remained over the years, but instead of a grocery store, it's been a counseling practice.

Next, ask God to reveal the gifting and talents He's given you that are designed to facilitate the fulfillment of your desires. Again, my gift of communication corresponds with my desire to write, broadcast, and counsel. They work together. It's my responsibility to steward this gift well by growing in my ability to communicate. This requires intentionality and purposeful growth, but it's all part of the process of stewarding the talent I've been given.

Consider the things that come naturally to you. What do you excel at? What do others say you do well? What would you do if money wasn't an issue? These are a few questions that can lead you down the path of discovering your gifting and talents. Ask God to reveal the talents you're currently unaware of, and ask Him to show you how you can grow them. Relentlessly pursue growth in the areas of your gifting.

Lastly, what is the world's greatest need as you see it? What is a problem for which you carry the unique solution? Where is the intersection for you, the place where your desires, talents, and the needs of others cross?

I asked these questions to Ashley recently. (I guess that's what you get when you're married to a counselor). I specifically asked her what she felt like *running* full stride for the glory of God looked like in her life. She paused as she considered her desires. I would later find out that she was having the following mental conversation:

> *Do I desire to write books like my husband and impact many people? No.*
> *Do I desire to broadcast the name of Jesus through the media like Gabe? No.*
> *Do I desire to counsel and help others discover the glory of God in their life? Not necessarily.*

She had kind of a sheepish smile, and with a hint of embarrassment in her voice, said, "I guess my deepest desires have always been to be a good mom." It was such a beautiful answer. I was quick to remind her that my desires were no more powerful than hers. After another pause, she said, "But how does my simple desire to be a mother bring great glory to God? It all seems so ordinary."

WE'RE NOT TERRORISTS

It was about six or seven days after that conversation that my heart started to race. I was quite nervous. It wasn't like we were stepping foot in a "Higgins" boat, preparing to storm the beaches of Normandy on D-Day. We weren't boarding the ill-fated Titanic. We were, however, on the precipice of what could be an extremely frightening situation—boarding a plane with three kids under the age of five.

Eyeballs locked on us like we were terrorists as we first made our way down the undersized aisle. Ashley was carrying our three-month-old drooling baby (Owen), and we also had our four-year-old (Avery) and two-year-old (Sophie) in tow. I noticed that people began fervently praying as we approached. I initially thought we were carrying a strong anointing, but then I realized people were praying that they wouldn't be stuck next to us. One older gentleman even said, "Keep walking." In that moment I realized we were "that" family.

We did keep walking—more like shuffling—as we made our way to aisles 25 and 26. Unfortunately, our seats were split between two separate rows (three in row 25 and one in row 26). Ashley displayed heroic courage as she said, "You sit behind us, and I'll sit here with the kids." She planted herself in the middle seat, placed Owen on her lap, and instructed Sophie to sit on her left and Avery on her right. I watched from a safe distance as one person after the next walked by and did a double take. I also witnessed others sitting near us, who apparently were stuck with the bad luck stick, each pull out their saucer-like headphones. I guess they came prepared.

I could have pulled out my own headphones and slipped into "nap land," however, better judgment prevailed as I remembered I didn't desire to sleep in the garage or live a life of married celibacy. I poked my head over the seat every few minutes, at first asking how I could help, and then just trying to catch a glimpse of *greatness*. I was in awe of watching Ashley navigate the situation. She looked like she had eight arms as she changed diapers, pulled out snacks, gently stroked the side of Sophie's face, picked up Owen's pacifier after it had fallen for the hundredth time, and even found time to hand me some food through the cracks of the seats. What a gal.

There were moments when the kids teetered on the verge of a breakdown, but Ashley pulled hard on the yoke each time to prevent the spiraling nosedive. She knew just what to do at the right time. People continued to stare, but I think she was slowly but surely winning the affection of those in the surrounding rows.

She had certainly won the affection of the man sitting in the row behind her. I couldn't stop thanking God for creating such an incredible woman as I continued to watch her love our children. I even thought to myself: *How does she do it? How is what I'm witnessing even possible for one person?* It was clear that I was watching a woman do what she was born to do. She was running full stride in her sweet spot, and it was indeed a glorious sight.

I wasn't the only one praising God on that plane. Everyone in the surrounding rows carried the same expression: *Thank God those kids aren't screaming in my ears.* See, Ashley? What you do does glorify God.

WHERE ARE YOU IN THE PROCESS?

As a young girl, Ashley carried a dream to be a mom. Her early childhood years were filled with scenes of a little girl with braids walking around the house carrying a baby doll. This desire was firmly established at a very young age. At the same time, she had to wait for the right timing before her desire would manifest into reality. She had to allow the process of maturation to run its course. Isn't the process of waiting a really good thing? I'm glad six-year-olds carrying baby dolls around because they have a desire to mother and nurture aren't actually afforded the opportunity to have kids while they're in the first grade!

I had to endure the process of maturation and wait for the right timing with my desires, too—and I'm still waiting for many. In order to be a counselor, I had to actually go to school and write the papers and take the tests. For a man who wanted to start building a practice and help people, school felt a little restrictive at times, kind of like a horse racing stall.

Because horses were born to run, they often have a difficult time walking into the starting gate at the beginning of the race. How often have you seen a horse bucking wildly behind the starting stalls, resisting the tiny gate with all its might? The obvious reality is that if a horse wants to enjoy the race, it has to momentarily step into something that seems very restrictive and uncomfortable.

The starting stall of a horse race serves as a useful illustration for understanding why we may not be seeing our desires come to pass—yet. God wants to see you *run*, which in this illustration means that He wants to fulfill your desires and give you the opportunity to do what you were created to do. At the same time, I think it's important to consider one of five possible scenarios for why it may not feel like the gate is opening.

First, God may be training and preparing you for your future race. Like any good trainer, there is a process that needs to happen before you are ready to really run. Horses want to run, so they probably think the shoeing process is really lame. Detailed preparation is a necessity for champion racehorses, and God takes the process of preparing us extremely seriously. He refuses to take shortcuts in the process of preparing you to *run*.

When I was twenty-five, I had a strong desire to get married. I wanted to experience the joy of marriage, so I prayed countless prayers asking God to "help a guy out." I specifically remember lying down to take a nap one Sunday afternoon when I felt a prompting to get up, go buy some food, and take it to a park in our city where many homeless people regularly gathered. I had just finished a busy morning of ministry, and going to feed the hungry was the last thing I felt like doing. I just sensed God watching me, waiting to see how I would respond to His prompting.

After I picked up the food and started driving to the park, I heard the familiar whisper of God: *Gabe, I hear your prayers for a wife. I am preparing you to be able to handle the responsibility. If you want a wife, you better get used to doing things you don't feel like doing.*

Looking back, I see the truth of His words. God was very interested in giving me the desire of my heart, but He also wanted to make sure I could handle the blessing well. If He would have given me a wife before I was ready, my selfishness could have done great damage to the relationship. Timing was important, and when I was ready, He came through in miraculous fashion.

Second, have you actually stepped into the starting stall? I've heard many people communicate a frustration with God's slow timing, but good questions to ask are: "What was the last thing God told you to do? Did you do it?" If you haven't done the last thing God asked you to do, you are like the horse that refuses to enter the gate. All the while, God is saying, *Trust me. I want to fulfill your desires, but you need to obey and enter the stall.*

The third possibility is that He may be working in the hearts of other people who are connected to the fulfillment of your desire. In horse racing, the gates don't open until all of the horses are in the stalls and ready. With my desire to get married, God was also working on Ashley and getting her ready. When we were both ready, God swung the gate wide open. I'm sure God has called people to run alongside you, but God wants to open the gate when everyone is ready. A good exercise is to pray for the people attached to the fulfillment of your desire, even if you don't know them by name.

The fourth possibility is that you are waiting for Him to open a gate that He doesn't desire to open. Essentially, you may be wanting to run on the wrong track. Hypothetically, let's say that I desire to be a rock star. Now, if you've ever heard me sing, you would understand this is certainly hypothetical. Imagine I start praying and praying for my big break, but the door never opens. Instead, other doors open and different opportunities present themselves, but I still really want to be an idolized rock star. I want to see my name in lights, not to mention enjoying the seven figure income that is common to that lifestyle. I may be disappointed that God is not giving me this opportunity, but in reality, it just means He has a better track for me to run on. James says it this way: *You do not have because you do not ask God. When you ask, you do not receive, because you ask with wrong motives, that you may spend what you get on your pleasures* (James 4:3, NIV). God may not be opening the door because He wants to protect you from running off the cliff.

Finally, the gate may be open already and God is simply waiting for you to step out of the stall! Perhaps fear or uncertainty is keeping you in the starting gate, but God wants to see you *arise and shine* and display to the dark world what He's placed in you.

Allow God to reveal if you fit into any of these categories. Is He just asking you to wait longer while He continues to prepare you? Have you done the last thing He asked you to do? Is He working *behind the scenes* as He prepares others that are also affiliated with the fulfillment of your desire? Are you waiting for a door to open that He doesn't want to open? Or, has He already opened the door and He's waiting for you to run?

Your present circumstance may be different than mine, but the common thread is that God desires to see us run. It's what we were born to do. For when we run, we bring Him glory.

SECTION IV
DEEP AND LIVING WATERS OF THE SPIRIT

Come, all you who are thirsty, come to the waters.
(Isaiah 55:1, NIV)

15.
SUBMERSION

There's something else that's extremely important and needed before we can truly *run* for the glory of God. It's the same thing the disciples needed before God *swung open the gate* and allowed them to run in pursuit of the Great Commission. They first needed to experience the deeper water of the Holy Spirit, the power of God within and upon them.

After the resurrection, Jesus appeared to the disciples on numerous occasions. On the day of His ascension, He handed the baton to them and commissioned them with mission and purpose. He said:

> *All authority has been given to Me in heaven and on earth. Go therefore and make disciples of all the nations, baptizing them in the name of the Father and the Son and the Holy Spirit, teaching them to observe all that I commanded you; and lo, I am with you always, even to the end of the age.* (Matthew 28:18-20, NASB)

Their calling was clear. The mandate had been given. But Jesus didn't give them the green light right away. Instead, He essentially ushered them into the starting gate as He told them to go to Jerusalem and wait for the gift the Father had promised. It was a classic, "Ready, set, ggg . . . wait!"

It's interesting to note that Jesus had already given them the Holy Spirit. He made quite a scene as He appeared in the room that had been bolted shut.

So when it was evening on that day, the first day of the week, and when the doors were shut where the disciples were, for fear of the Jews, Jesus came and stood in their midst and said to them, "Peace be with you." And when He had said this, He showed them both His hands and His side. The disciples then rejoiced when they saw the Lord. So Jesus said to them again, "Peace be with you; as the Father has sent Me, I also send you." And when He had said this, He breathed on them and said to them, "Receive the Holy Spirit." (John 20:19-22, NASB)

If Jesus didn't actually give them the Holy Spirit when He breathed upon them, this would have been an extremely awkward scenario. It would have been more like a Mentos commercial. The fact is they did receive the Spirit when He breathed upon them. So why would Jesus then ask them to go and continue to wait for something they already had? There must have been more He wanted to give them.

Jesus' intention was for the Spirit to not only abide within the disciples, but He wanted them to be completely submersed in this life-giving and empowering "water"—the Holy Spirit. Jesus actually put it this way: *Do not leave Jerusalem until the Father sends you the gift he promised, as I told you before. John baptized with water, but in just a few days you will be baptized with the Holy Spirit* (Acts 1:4-5, NLT).

The Greek word used for "baptism" is "baptizo," which means, "to dip repeatedly, to immerse, to submerge." It's the same word used to reference sunken vessels. This is not a teaspoon dosage or a sprinkling. Picture the *Titanic* sitting deep in the frigid waters of the North Atlantic, completely immersed in water. Years of submersion have obviously negatively affected the condition of the ship, but the opposite is true for us with the immersion of the Spirit. The more we allow God to submerge us in the life-giving waters of the Spirit, the better our lives will function and the more victory and freedom we'll experience. As Paul declared, *Where the Spirit of the Lord is there is liberty* (2 Corinthians 3:17, NASB). Not to mention our powerful lives and ministries will help others attain the same victory and freedom as a result of the Spirit at work through us.

This immersion of the Spirit that the disciples were waiting for was termed by Jesus as a "gift from the Father." Remember how generous the Father is? We see His generosity again in Acts 2:

> *On the day of Pentecost all the believers were meeting together in one place. Suddenly, there was a sound from heaven like the roaring of a*

mighty windstorm, and it filled the house where they were sitting. Then, what looked like flames or tongues of fire appeared and settled on each of them. And everyone present was filled with the Holy Spirit and began speaking in other languages, as the Holy Spirit gave them this ability.
(Acts 2:1-4, NLT)

Flames of fire on their heads? Speaking in unknown languages? This is where some people get a little spooked. It all seems so mysterious and . . . strange. Is this really in the Bible? This fear of mystery causes many to stop their journey into the deeper waters of the Spirit. This is also where the enemy whispers: "Don't go there. You'll be one of the weird ones. Stay in the shallow, comfortable waters, the place where you can maintain control but still call yourself a Christian." That sounds awfully familiar to me.

There is real spiritual opposition to you receiving the power of the Holy Spirit. The spiritual war that rages is about territory and the advancement of kingdoms, and "power" is a priceless commodity in this cosmic battle. The enemy has a decidedly large disadvantage in the area of power (Jesus said, "All authority has been given to Me . . . "), so Satan works extra hard to discount the opportunity for you to receive the power of God.

I was reminded of this reality as I started working on this chapter. I've faced more spiritual resistance in working on this chapter than all of the others combined. A variety of thoughts have popped into my mind: *Go with the funny stories. Don't talk about the power of the Spirit or people will lose interest.* I was able to take these thoughts captive and recognize their origin—the father of lies. I then reminded myself that this is not about entertaining people. It's about declaring the message that God desires for us to live powerful lives in the Holy Spirit! This is not just for the people who attend churches with crazy music and lights, it's for normal everyday Christ followers.

WHAT SHOULD A NORMAL CHRISTIAN LIFE LOOK LIKE?

The real issue at hand has nothing to do with whether you'll be labeled "weird" as you venture deeper into the Spirit. Nor is it about which side is right in the ongoing theological debate about Spirit baptism. The real question is, "What should the normal Christian life look like?" This is a crucial question to ask. Who set the original example of what our lives should look like? Jesus Himself. What was Jesus' interaction with the Holy Spirit?

One day when the crowds were being baptized, Jesus himself was baptized. As he was praying, the heavens opened, and the Holy Spirit, in bodily form, descended on him like a dove. And a voice from heaven said, "You are my dearly loved Son, and you bring me great joy." (Luke 3:21-22, NLT)

Jesus was clothed with the same powerful Holy Spirit that He offers us today. It was the power that fueled and enabled His ministry. It was the power that empowered Him to proclaim good news to the poor, bind up the brokenhearted, and offer freedom for the oppressed.

Some may think, *Yes, but that's Jesus. I'm not Jesus.* That's true. However, doesn't He live within you? Don't you have access to the same Spirit? Didn't He even say on the night of His crucifixion that His disciples would do greater things than He? (John 14:12). Don't we have access to the same Holy Spirit those miracle working disciples had? Our excuses for why we lack power don't hold water. This is actually good news though, because a life without power is a life of defeat and bondage—the opposite of what we were created to experience.

I stood on a beach half a world away in India when a pastor asked me if I had experienced the deeper waters of the Holy Spirit. I was quick to resist, and the images playing through my mind were those I had seen on television, of people seemingly putting on a show as they dramatically fell to the ground after being touched by the Holy Spirit. And besides, I said to myself, *I've already received Jesus into my heart. I have the Holy Spirit.*

I was right. I had the Holy Spirit. I was also wrong. There was more that God wanted me to experience. In my ignorance, I assumed I knew everything there was to know about the gift of the Spirit. After the pastor walked me through several Scriptures that addressed the topic of the Spirit (many of which I described above), I decided I didn't just want this gift, I actually needed this gift. Being filled and submersed in the Spirit is what distinguishes us as the people of God. It's the thing that empowers us to love and serve others well. (The first "fruit" of the Spirit mentioned in Galatians 5 is love.)

In fact, in the first church we see the apostles choosing people who were "filled with the Spirit and wisdom" to serve and oversee the daily distribution of food (Acts 6). Being filled with the Spirit isn't just for those who are on the speaking circuit, it's for all who serve in the body of Christ. It's for all who call themselves Christ followers.

The pastor (who was also becoming my new friend) placed his hands on my shoulder and prayed for the deep waters of the Spirit to sweep over me. It was a surreal place for this prayer to be offered, because in the natural, I heard the crashing of the ocean's waves a few feet from where I was standing. I felt something similar happening in the spiritual sense as I felt the waves of His Spirit crashing upon me. This was a turning point in my life and for my ministry. I simply discovered that I would never find the "ocean floor" when it comes to the deep water of the Spirit. There will always be more that God wants to unveil.

Over the years I've also learned that the Holy Spirit isn't weird. We are the weird ones. Not everything that you've seen done in the name of the Holy Spirit was a result of the actual Spirit working in people's lives. At the same time, we can't build a box around the Spirit and assume He'll only work according to our expectations and guidelines. We have to leave Him plenty of room to surprise us. Let's allow Him to express Himself the way He desires. Trying to control and manipulate the Spirit to avoid "weirdness" is a sure way to inhibit His full expression in our lives.

THE CONTINUAL INVITATION TO GO DEEPER

I'm sitting in my office, praying through this chapter, and I still sense God saying, *There's more.* He's drawing me deeper. This is not just theory that I'm trying to get you to buy into. This is an even deeper reality I am being invited into.

The power of the Holy Spirit in your life is the thing that separates religion as mere theory from actually putting the truths of the sacred Scriptures into practice on a daily basis. Richard Foster writes:

> The perpetual presence of the Lord moves from a theological dogma into a radiant reality. "He walks with me and he talks with me" ceases to be pious jargon and instead becomes a straightforward description of daily life.1

You were designed to take territory for the kingdom of God, and this requires operating in the power that God freely gives. I find myself often praying a simple prayer: "God, I want all of the power you desire to give me. I want all of the Holy Spirit that you desire for me to experience. Bring it on, Jesus." This cuts through some of the endless theological debates on the Holy Spirit—and the need to prove ourselves correct on the issue—and it takes the question directly to the Father. If you genuinely ask for all that He has to give you, then you're leaving the decision in His hands. Your role is to simply ask, seek, and knock. Jesus' words from Luke 11 give us a pretty good indication of what His answer will be:

> *So I say to you, ask, and it will be given to you; seek, and you will find; knock, and it will be opened to you. For everyone who asks, receives; and he who seeks, finds; and to him who knocks, it will be opened. Now suppose one of you fathers is asked by his son for a fish; he will not give him a snake instead of a fish, will he? Or if he is asked for an egg, he will not give him a scorpion, will*

he? If you then, being evil, know how to give good gifts to your children, how much more will your heavenly Father give the Holy Spirit to those who ask Him? (Luke 11: 9-13, NASB)

Not only are you blessed in this process of asking for an increased measure of the Spirit, but the countless lives of other people God has called you to impact for the kingdom of God need you to operate with the power of the Spirit. There's too much at stake to live lives void of any real power. People are perishing, and they desperately need Christians—the ones who actually have the answer—to arise and demonstrate this glorious answer with power.

It's one thing for me to say these things, but it's much more powerful for you to actually hear it yourself from God. Ask the Father if there's more of the gift of the Spirit that He desires for you to experience.

Ask the Father to give you a picture of where you are currently in your relationship with the Holy Spirit. For example, are you in ankle-deep water? Knee-deep water? I asked Him this question and He was quick to answer. I then asked Him where He wanted to take me, and He said, *I don't want you to even be able to see the shore.*

What's He saying to you? Are you willing to allow Him to make this a reality?

Jesus, I believe the Scripture when it states that you are the one who baptizes in the Holy Spirit. I also believe that this is a gift from the Heavenly Father. I ask not for a sprinkling but for a complete immersion in your Spirit. I believe you made it abundantly clear that the Spirit is crucial for the fulfillment of my calling, and I want all that you desire to give me. Let your Spirit sweep over me and lead me into continual, deeper waters. Thank you for this tremendous gift. Amen.

16.
THE TREASURE WITHIN

Where does the rubber actually meet the road? This all sounds good, but what does it look like on a daily basis in your life? What does it look like to live a Spirit-filled, Spirit-empowered life on a Monday morning when you sit at your desk and stare at a stack of work that needs to be done? What does it look like on a Thursday morning, when you're about to pull out your hair because your young kids have been whining for the past few hours? What does it look like on a Saturday morning as you sit at the same coffee shop you've gone to for years? How do you really take the idea of living an extraordinary life so submersed in the Spirit that you *can't see the shore* and actually apply it to everyday life (a life that often seems very ordinary and at times, boring)?

While I can't pretend to tell you exactly what it should look like in your unique life circumstances, I do know a God who will personally reveal it to you. I can tell you He is passionate about invading your ordinary day with His extraordinary Spirit. This doesn't mean the tower of work documents calling for your attention will disappear. Nor will your kids instantly stop whining. Perhaps you'll still show up at the same coffee shop for the next several years, but you won't be alone. You'll be filled and surrounded with the greatest power the world has ever known.

Not only is He constantly with us, but He constantly wants to be involved in the details of our lives. He wants to help. He wants to fulfill His purposes. He wants to express Himself through you to your ordinary surroundings and the seemingly ordinary people who surround you. In order for this to happen, you have to renew your mind and walk with a continual awareness of His presence. We must not neglect this great treasure as we go about our day.

BURIED AND FORGOTTEN TREASURE

In 2007, an Austrian man named Andreas K. was working on expanding his backyard pond when he stumbled upon some items buried underground. Not knowing the true value of the items he uncovered, he placed them in a box and stored them in his basement.

In 2009, after packing his house and preparing to move, Andreas once again came across the formerly buried treasure in his basement. The items were still encrusted in dirt, but some of the soil had since hardened and fallen off, revealing something he had not seen hundreds of days prior: precious metal and jewels.

He initially determined to place the items for sale online, but instead, after collectors alerted Andreas of their true value, he loaded up his newly discovered treasure and took it to Austrian authorities to allow them to evaluate its estimated worth.

They were shocked. The Austrian Federal Office of Memorials released a statement that read, in part: "Fairy tales still exist!" and "Private individual finds sensational treasure in his backyard." The statement went on to label the discovery "one of the qualitatively most significant discoveries of medieval treasure in Austria."

If Andreas had understood the true value of the items stored away in his basement, he wouldn't have forgotten about them. He wouldn't have allowed multiple birthdays to pass while the treasure sat and collected dust under his own roof. He would have been more like the person Jesus described in Matthew 13:

*The kingdom of heaven is like treasure hidden in a field. When a man found it, he hid it again, and then in his joy went and sold all he had and bought that field. (*Matthew 13:44, NIV)

We have a treasure within us that is of greater worth than gold and rubies. Paul writes, *We now have this light shining in our hearts, but we ourselves are like fragile clay jars containing this great treasure. This makes it clear that our great power is from God, not from ourselves* (2 Corinthians 4:7, NLT).

How easy is it to allow the busyness of the day to distract our attention and cause us to forget about the treasure under own roofs—the Spirit in us? Like Andreas, it's usually because we don't understand His real worth and value. We don't grasp how much He really wants to be engaged on a daily basis.

Look again at the second part of the verse: "This makes it clear that our great power is from God, not from ourselves." Is it clear on a typical day that you are operating in the power of the Spirit rather than your own power? This is a sobering thought to consider.

We're talking about the same powerful Spirit who raised Jesus from the dead; the same power that opened the eyes of the blind and cured the man with leprosy in the Gospels. It's the same power that I needed exerted into my body as I lay in a hospital bed suffering from kidney failure a few years ago.

I was in a lot of pain as they wheeled me into a tiny little room that carried an anything but tiny smell. I looked over to see that I had a roommate, a man in his eighties who was suffering from gastrointestinal issues. We were separated by a small curtain, which did little to keep the sounds and smells on his side of the room. If the kidney failure didn't do me in, the stench in the room was about to.

Thankfully, I had family and friends who were willing to enter the fog, place their hands on me, and pray for the power of the Holy Spirit to heal my body. A few days later, the doctor literally said: "This is miraculous. I'm not sure how you got better, but you did. We are going to release you today."

"Yes, you're right," I said with a smile. "It was miraculous."

Whether you are praying for the sick, sharing the good news of the Gospel, serving coffee at Starbucks, teaching in a classroom, or raising children, the power, grace, love, patience, and kindness of the Holy Spirit wants to be engaged and released through your life.

It's amazing how much better things work when we allow God to be God in the details of our lives. Let Him guide your budget decisions. Allow Him to teach you to be a better parent. Invite Him to flood you with creative ideas for your workplace. Allow His power to flow through you to heal the sick. Let Him do all this for His glory, not yours. People will begin to recognize that you are operating in a power that surpasses your own ability. They'll look beyond the clay jar and see the treasure you possess.

This doesn't mean you sit cross-legged on the floor during work meetings while uttering meditative chants, but it means you possess an awareness of His presence as you engage your coworkers in the meeting. You allow Him to whisper to your heart. You ask Him for His opinion. You respond to the promptings He gives. You simply pay attention to what He's up to while simultaneously paying attention to what's happening in the meeting.

I once had breakfast with a man who was frustrated by the spiritual apathy he thought his daughter displayed. "Gabe," he said while shaking his head, "I've tried everything and I don't know how to reach this girl. Nothing is working." He paused and looked down at the table while his mind continued to search for answers. I asked, "Have you asked the Holy Spirit how He's pursuing her?"

This was a man who had just graduated from a Bible college that actively taught on the power and activity of the Holy Spirit. He was a man who was very much in tune with the Spirit on a regular basis, but he still looked surprised by my question. "No, I guess I haven't," he admitted in a moment of honesty. "I guess I probably should."

"Well you are obviously passionate about reaching your daughter," I said, "and God is far more passionate about her than you are. I'm willing to bet He's already actively pursuing her." A look of relief flashed across his face. I continued, "Find out what the Holy Spirit is doing and cooperate with Him. Let Him express Himself through you to your precious daughter." He left much more encouraged than when he arrived. I've since watched this same girl grow dramatically in her faith. Apparently, the Spirit not only pursued her, but He captured her little heart.

BEYOND NATURAL ABILITY

I often pray fervently before counseling sessions. Many of my clients are much older than I am, so I need to lean into a greater source of wisdom than I naturally possess. One older woman who arrived for her first counseling session was visibly surprised at my apparent youth. She pinched my cheek (which I didn't enjoy), and said, "You're old enough to be my grandson." (Translation: "Am I wasting my time with someone who appears to be so young? What wisdom do you have to offer a woman twice your age?")

A few weeks into the counseling process, she looked at me with tears in her eyes and said: "You saved my life. I am a completely different woman because of our sessions together." I'm only saying this to explain that she was experiencing the power and wisdom of the Holy Spirit working through me. It was power and wisdom that went beyond my natural ability. I was quick to give credit where credit was due, and I used it as an opportunity to talk to her about God's boundless love towards her.

I was praying before a session recently when the Spirit spoke to my heart: *Gabe, don't complicate this process. Let me be myself to my people through you.* God was reminding me that it wasn't my job to provide all of the answers and healing. (Yes, I do believe it's important to be trained and skilled in the profession of counseling, however, my first responsibility is to allow Him to work through me.) The result has been that I've often felt like I'm on the front row, watching the Spirit do some amazing work.

The other day, I piled into my little car after a long day of counseling and prepared to head home. I was tired, but I was also energized from all that God had done. I smiled, and said: "That was impressive, God. You're really good at this."

How does the Holy Spirit want to express Himself through you today? He wants to be Himself to His people through you. How does He specifically want to show others that your power is coming from Him instead of you?

This can happen in a variety of ways: When you feel your patience wearing thin, lean into the patience of the Spirit. When you feel like your work meetings aren't accomplishing anything, lean into the wisdom and creativity of the Spirit. When you aren't sure you can tackle another load of laundry, lean into the strength of the Spirit. When you're standing over a sick and suffering person in a stink-filled hospital room . . . plug your nose and lean into the power of the Holy Spirit.

17.
TRULY SATISFYING

The Spirit of God doesn't *just* clothe you with power; He also satisfies the deep thirst of the soul. He is the water that truly satisfies. Listen to the passion of God's invitation through the prophet Isaiah:

> *Come, all you who are thirsty,*
>   *come to the waters;*
> *and you who have no money,*
>   *come, buy and eat!*
> *Come, buy wine and milk*
>   *without money and without cost.*
> *Why spend money on what is not bread,*
>   *and your labor on what does not satisfy?*
> *Listen, listen to me, and eat what is good,*
>   *and you will delight in the richest of fare.*
> (Isaiah 55:1-2, NIV)

Who would turn down this invitation? Who doesn't want to be satisfied at a deep level? This is what we all look for, but some just know where to look in order to find this satisfying water.

OFF THE BEATEN PATH

At one point in my life, I worked on a department team of all women. In addition, I also provided counseling services at a women's medical clinic. When I went home in the evening, I saw my beautiful bride and two daughters. It goes without saying that I was surrounded by a lot of estrogen. This is precisely why my man-heart nearly leaped out of my chest when a buddy approached me and said, "I'm going fly fishing in a few weeks. Wanna go?"

Our fishing trip was like a cold glass of water for my soul. We drove ATVs up the rugged mountain trail, surrounded by some of the finest views on the planet. Our final destination was a little mountain lake that possessed clear water and large trout. It was snuggled between multiple peaks at the top of the Sangre de Cristo Mountains. We were probably halfway to the top when Rick pulled his ATV off to the side of the trail and said, "Follow me."

We hacked our way through tall grass and pokey bushes as he explained that a man who once lived in the area let him in on a little secret. "Somewhere in this vicinity," he said with a look of excitement, "is a pipe connected to a natural spring that flows from the belly of the earth." He paused, and then emphatically said, "It'll be the best water you've ever tasted."

We found the pipe, but we were disappointed to learn that it was dry as a bone. Rick looked confused. "We've come up here for years, and it's never been dry." One of the other guys followed the pipe back up the hill and discovered that the spring of water was flowing just as much as ever, but the pipe had been disconnected from the water supply. After reconnecting the pipe, we took turns filling and refilling our containers with this incredible water. It was an endless supply of cold, pure, satisfying aquae. And hardly anyone knew it was available.

The only water I've tasted that's been more satisfying is the water of the Spirit, the water Jesus offers. And, sadly, we live in a culture where too few people know it exists. Most people stay on the beaten trail, and ride right on by the spring of living water. They're not willing to respond to Jesus' invitation to "follow me" and hack through the tall grass and pokey bushes. They miss out.

Jesus never meant for this water to be a secret. He didn't try and hide this well from others. In fact, He offered it freely to the Samaritan woman in John 4.

It was the heat of the day, and Jesus was probably dog-tired. In the midst of traveling from Judea to Galilee, He decided to sit down and rest at a well. At the same time, a woman approached the well looking for a little water, but she was about to hear of something far better than H$_2$0.

There came a woman of Samaria to draw water. Jesus said to her, "Give Me a drink." For His disciples had gone away into the city to buy food. Therefore the Samaritan woman said to Him, "How is it that You, being a Jew, ask me for a drink since I am a Samaritan woman?" (For Jews have no dealings with Samaritans.) Jesus answered and said to her, "If you knew the gift of God, and who it is who says to you, 'Give Me a drink,' you would have asked Him, and He would have given you living water." She said to Him, "Sir, You have nothing to draw with and the well is deep; where then do You get that living water? You are not greater than our father Jacob, are You, who gave us the well, and drank of it himself and his sons and his cattle?" Jesus answered and said to her, "Everyone who drinks of this water will thirst again; but whoever drinks of the water that I will give him shall never thirst; but the water that I will give him will become in him a well of water springing up to eternal life." (John 4:7-14, NASB)

I'm sure the woman initially gave Jesus a perplexed look, but she eventually became a believer and a witness for Christ. The Scripture goes on to explain that many Samaritans also believed because of her testimony. We can only assume that she eventually received this living water and found the ultimate satisfaction.

Jesus continued to offer this same invitation to others. In John 7, we see Him pleading at the top of His lungs for people to receive this gift.

Now on the last day, the great day of the feast, Jesus stood and cried out, saying, "If anyone is thirsty, let him come to Me and drink." (John 7:37, NASB)

I'm sure His brothers cringed as they watched Him make such a scene. How would you respond if your brother or sister were to stand up at church this Sunday and cry out loudly? Would it be a little uncomfortable? Jesus doesn't care what anyone thinks. He is so passionate about revealing the gift of God that He stands to his feet, opens His mouth, and lets it rip! He knows that if people will simply respond to the invitation, they will find the very thing they were created for. They'll taste of the only water that can quench their thirst. He continued:

> He who believes in Me, as the Scripture said, "From his innermost being will flow rivers of living water." (John 7:38, NASB)

What a beautiful picture. Jesus wants us to drink deeply of the Spirit and then allow the same Spirit to flow from us to others. This is precisely what Christian living is supposed to look like. We are to be satisfied by the water Jesus offers, and then we are to offer the same water to others.

We don't force it, manipulate it, or manufacture it, but it happens because we're simply connected to the spring. The pipe is hooked up to the true source—Jesus.

The way we connect to Jesus isn't complicated. It's not a mysterious formula. It's about simply developing an intimate relationship with Him. Jesus said, "Come to me and drink." There are no strings attached, no hoops to jump through, and no "three easy payments of only $19.99." The invitation in Isaiah was to "come buy wine and milk without money and without cost." It's waiting for us. He's waiting for us.

THE SECRET PLACE

We've covered a lot of topics in this book, but it all boils down to the importance of knowing Jesus Christ. Our primary calling is to develop intimacy with Him, to love Him with all of our heart, soul, mind, and strength. There are no words that can adequately describe the passion of His heart for us. All we're left to do is draw near and "taste and see."

Moving forward, He wants to establish a secret place in our hearts where we meet with Him often. It's the place where "deep calls to deep." From this place, a beautiful intimacy will develop, resulting in a stream of living water that will flow from within us. Others will taste of this water and be inspired to develop their own secret place with Jesus. They'll desire to know the same Jesus you and I know. Then water will flow from their hearts, too. On and on it goes until the deep water of the glory of God covers the earth. It all starts from a place of sweet intimacy with Jesus.

This book actually started from that same place. After I discovered many years ago that Jesus is deeply relational, I started engaging Him in conversation and recording our dialogue. I sat in front of my computer for hours upon hours typing out my thoughts to Him and then typing out what I thought He was saying in response. Sometimes tears rolled off my cheeks and saturated my keyboard. Other times I laughed, deeply. And yet, there were other times when I just sat in silence and let Him give me that bear hug. It was time well spent with a pretty amazing friend. I recorded thousands of pages of conversation, and the two most common things I heard Him say were:

I love you.
Come closer.

He did say something several years ago that caught me off guard though. While I had assumed my typical posture of listening and typing, He said: *You're writing a book right now.*

"A book?" I asked. "I'm not writing a book, I'm journaling and talking to you. Besides, this is our secret place. This isn't for others to read." I gave Him my own look of perplexity. I think He just smiled...and winked.

I guess He was right, after all. And He just said it:

I told you so.

ACKNOWLEDGMENTS

My deep thanks to my wife, Ashley, for offering unwavering love and support throughout this journey. She was heroic. Thank you to my children for being patient and gracious while I spent extra time in the "cave" writing. Thank you to my parents for consistently demonstrating the love and faithfulness of Christ over the years. Also, thanks to Jim and Janelle for their hard work and commitment to excellence throughout the editing and design process. And thank you to the many friends who read the manuscript and offered feedback and encouragement along the way: Colen, David, Connie, Abby, Dale, Doug, Steve, Reid, Bobby, Connie, Jarred, Thomas, and Joyce. This certainly wasn't a solo project.

Notes:

Introduction:
1. Richard J. Foster, Celebration of Discipline: The Path to Spiritual Growth (New York, NY, Harper Collins Publishers, 1998) page 2.

Chapter 6:
1. Kenneth Bailey, The Cross and the Prodigal: Luke 15 Through the Eyes of Middle Eastern Peasants (Downers Grove, IL: Intervarsity Press) page 52.

Chapter 8:
1. George MacDonald, "Man's Difficulty Concerning Prayer," in Creation in Christ, ed. Rolland Hein (Wheaton, Ill.: Harold Shaw, 197), pp. 329-30.

Chapter 9:
1. http://www.imsdb.com/scripts/Lion-King,-The.pdf (Lion King Script)
2. Brennan Manning, Abba's Child (Colorado Springs, Co: NAVPRESS, 1994) page 21.
3. Henri Nouwen, The Way of the Heart (New York: Ballantine Publishing Group, 1981) pages 10-11.
4. John Eldredge, Wild at Heart (Nashville, Tn: Thomas Nelson, Inc., 2001) page 8.

Chapter 10:
1. Brennan Manning, Abba's Child (Colorado Springs, Co: NAVPRESS, 1994) page 21.

Chapter 12:
1. John Eldredge, Wild at Heart (Nashville, Tn: Thomas Nelson, Inc., 2001) page 127.

Chapter 14:
1. Lawerence Scanlan, The Horse God Built: The Untold Story of Secretariat, the World's Greatest Racehorse (New York, NY: St. Martin's Press, 2007) page 44.
2. Scanlan, p. 44.
3. John Eldredge, Wild at Heart (Nashville, Tn: Thomas Nelson, Inc., 2001) page 9.

Chapter 15:
1. Richard J. Foster, Celebration of Discipline: The Path to Spiritual Growth (New York, NY, Harper Collins Publishers, 1998) page 19.